SPIRITUAL GIFTS

MINISTRIES AND MANIFESTATIONS

B. E. UNDERWOOD

Published by
LIFESPRINGS RESOURCES
Franklin Springs, Georgia 30639

ISBN # Paper Edition: 0-911866-03-5

Preface

The basic material in this book has been developed over a period of about 20 years. In 1967, after several years of intensive study of spiritual gifts, I published a book entitled *The Gifts of the Spirit—Supernatural Equipment for Christian Service.* That publication, which has been translated into Spanish and Korean, deals with the nine manifestation gifts listed in 1 Corinthians 12. In its writing, I made no effort to address the broader subject of spiritual gifts.

Since that time, many excellent books have been written on this subject. Most of these works, however, make no distinction between ministry gifts and manifestation gifts. The tendency is to confuse these two kinds of spiritual gifts. The need to clarify this distinction led to the preparation of this book.

The commentary presented in this book was developed in connection with a teaching assignment at the Centre for International Christian Ministries (CICM) in London, England. My thanks go to the staff and students at CICM for their encouragement and assistance in the compilation of this course. It also has been my privilege to teach these lectures around the world in local churches, pastors' seminars, and in schools of missions.

This book has now been published in five languages and is being used around the world to sharpen the understanding of God's people with regard to spiritual gifts. May He continue to use it for His purposes.

Unless noted otherwise, biblical quotations are from the King James Version.

To avoid clumsiness in reading, the masculine pronouns will be used in antecedent agreement.

—B. E. Underwood

Contents

Preface..5

1. Ministry or Manifestation?.....................................9

2. Equipping Ministry Gifts......................................19

3. The Fourfold Task of the Shepherd......................31

4. Body Ministry Gifts...41

5. Harmonizing the Gifts 51

6. Manifestation Gifts 63

7. The Initial Evidence of the
   Fullness of the Spirit 73

8. Three Kinds of Tongues 83

9. Guidelines for Spiritual Manifestations 93

10. The Greatest Hindrance—The Flesh 103

11. The Atmosphere of the Gifts—
    The Fruit of the Spirit 113

12. The Most Important Ingredient in
    Spiritual Gifts—Love.......................................123

Bibliography...133

CHAPTER ONE

Ministry or Manifestation?

The classical Pentecostal Movement has been talking about spiritual gifts since 1906. But beginning about 1967 Christendom in general became increasingly interested in the subject.

To classical pentecostals, spiritual gifts were those manifestation gifts listed in 1 Corinthians 12.

Earlier interest in spiritual gifts failed to adequately recognize the ministry gifts, which are also gifts of the Spirit. Recent studies also have erred by not recognizing the distinction between ministry gifts and manifestation gifts, which are essential to the dynamic life and growth of the church.

Let us examine the lists of spiritual gifts as found in Romans 12:6-8; 1 Corinthians 12:4-11, 28; Ephesians 4:11; and 1 Peter 4:9-11.

First, in Romans 12:6-8 Paul writes, "Having then gifts differing according to the grace that is given to us, whether prophecy, let us prophesy according to the proportion of faith; Or ministry, let us wait on our ministering: or he that teacheth, on teaching; Or he that exhorteth, on exhortation: he that giveth, let him do it with simplicity; he that ruleth, with diligence; he that sheweth mercy, with cheerfulness."

Seven gifts are listed here: prophecy, ministry, teaching, exhortation, giving, ruling, and mercy. All of these are ministry gifts.

Then move on to 1 Corinthians 12:4-11. Here the apostle begins by saying, "Now there are diversities of gifts, but the same Spirit" (v. 4). In verse 7 he writes, "But the manifestation of the Spirit is given to every man to profit withal." He proceeds in verses 8-10 to list these manifestation gifts: "For to one is given by the Spirit the word of wisdom; to another the word of knowledge by the same Spirit; To another faith by the same Spirit; to another the gifts of healing by the same Spirit; To another the working of miracles; to another prophecy; to another discerning of spirits; to another divers kinds of tongues; to another the interpretation of tongues."

These nine manifestations of the Spirit are the gifts commonly recognized by classical pentecostals as "the gifts of the Spirit."

In Ephesians 4:11 we have another special kind of spiritual gift. In verse 8 Paul declares that the ascended Christ "gave gifts unto men." Then in verses 11-13 he writes, "It was he who gave some to be apostles, some to be prophets, some to be evangelists, and some to be pastors and teachers, to prepare God's people for works of service, so that the body of Christ may be built up until we all reach unity in the faith and in the knowledge of the Son of God and become mature, attaining to the whole measure of the fullness of Christ" (NIV).

Finally, in 1 Peter 4:10,11 we read, "Each one should use whatever gift he has received to serve others, faithfully administering God's grace in its various forms. If anyone speaks, he should do it as one speaking the very words of God. If anyone serves, he should do it with the strength God provides, so that in all things God may be praised through Jesus Christ. To whom be the glory and the power for ever and ever Amen" (NIV).

An understanding of these four passages is essential to any clear teaching on spiritual gifts. A key to this understanding must take into account the various words used in Scripture for "gift." The King James Version translates 12 different Hebrew words with the English word *gift*. It translates eight different Greek words by the word *gift,* or *gifts.* So when Paul writes, "There are diversities of gifts," he is focusing on an important facet of any study of spiritual gifts.

FOUR GREEK WORDS

Let us look at four of these words that are used in connection with spiritual gifts.

(1) *Charismata.*

The Greek word *charismata* comes from the root word *charis*, meaning grace. This is the term used in 1 Corinthians 12:4. It is also found in 1 Corinthians 12:31, Romans 12:6, and 1 Peter 4:10. *Charismata* seems to be a general term. It may be used of all spiritual gifts. As we are told in 1 Corinthians 12:4, there are different kinds of *charismata.*

(2) *Domata.*

The word *domata* is found only in Ephesians 4:8, and it refers to those leadership ministry gifts listed in Ephesians 4:11. *Domata* has to do with gifted men who are placed in the church for the equipping of the saints.

(3) *Dorea.*

Dorea is the usual Greek term for gifts. It is a root word from which several other words are derived. This word is used in Acts 2:38; 10:45; Ephesians 3:7; 4:7, as well as many other places.

(4) *Phanerosis.*

The word used in 1 Corinthians 12:7 is the Greek word *phanerosis.* It is a term meaning to lay bare, to unveil. It also means to shine forth, to reveal—reveal oneself. This is the word used for those gifts listed in 1 Corinthians 12:8-10. *Phanerosis* is the term used for those supernatural manifestations that I call the "surprises of the Spirit."

It seems clear that there are different kinds of spiritual gifts. While they all are gifts of God's grace, there are distinctions between them.

MINISTRY GIFTS

First, we must distinguish between ministry gifts and manifestation gifts. Then we must distinguish between two kinds of ministry gifts—*equipping ministry gifts and body ministry gifts.*

(1) Equipping Ministry Gifts.

The equipping ministry gifts are apostle, prophet, evangelist, and pastor-teacher (Ephesians 4:11). These are leadership gifts. They are individuals given to the church to equip her for her ministry.

(2) Body Ministry Gifts.

Next we will examine the body ministry gifts and deal with seven gifts in this category: (1) exhorter, (2) teacher, (3) helps (or service), (4) administration (or governments), (5) benevolence (or mercy), (6) giving, and (7) hospitality. We will not aim at being exhaustive in listing body ministry gifts. Our purpose is to point out certain principles concerning spiritual gifts and the distinction between the different kinds of gifts so that we may be able to understand better how the Holy Spirit operates in the church. Possibly all other body ministry gifts could be listed under one of these seven typical gifts.

MANIFESTATION GIFTS

The second major category of spiritual gifts includes the nine manifestation gifts listed in 1 Corinthians 12, which are: (1) a word of wisdom, (2) a word of knowledge, (3) faith, (4) gifts of healing (or healings), (5) working of miracles, (6) prophecy, (7) discerning of spirits, (8) tongues, and (9) interpretation of tongues. These manifestations of the Spirit *(phanerosis)* are those "surprises of the Spirit" which reveal His supernatural presence in the church. These manifestations are essential to the health and growth of the body of Christ.

Now let us review the various lists as they are given in the New Testament. The equipping ministry gifts are listed in Ephesians 4:11. This list deals solely with the equipping ministry gifts of the Spirit.

In Romans 12:6-8 all the gifts named are ministry gifts, including both equipping ministry gifts and body ministry gifts. In 1 Corinthians 12:6-8 Paul inventories only manifestation gifts. Later in the chapter (v. 28) he gives a list that includes all three kinds of spiritual gifts: "And in the church God has appointed first of all apostles, second prophets, third teachers, then workers of miracles, also those having gifts of healing, those able to help others, those with gifts of administration, and those speaking in different kinds of tongues" (NIV). Paul is doing two things in this passage. First, he is trying to help these charismatic Corinthians to put manifestation gifts in their proper perspective. He doesn't criticize them for having such demonstrations. Nowhere does he tell them to eradicate these manifestations. Rather, he forbids them to stop such manifestations (14:39).

The Corinthians had become so concerned with the spectacular manifestations of the Spirit that they had failed to put spiritual gifts in the proper perspective. So, here in this second list (12:28), he first names three equipping ministry gifts, and numbers them "first," "second," and "third." When he finishes the list, he says, "after that ... then ...." The "first," the "second," and the "third," indicate that all other spiritual gifts are to be in submission to the equipping ministry gifts. Both the body ministry gifts and the manifestation gifts are to be subject to those leadership gifts listed in Ephesians 4:11.

In this list (12:28) there are three equipping ministry gifts, three manifestation gifts, and two body ministry gifts. Paul makes no effort to give an exhaustive list of gifts here. His purpose is to bring perspective to the whole issue of spiritual gifts. He wants these Corinthians to see both the unity of the church and the diversity of spiritual gifts. Each member functions according to his gift or gifts, and at the proper time and place in the church. Paul is leading these charismatic Corinthians into a proper understanding of the manifestations of the Spirit as they relate to other spiritual gifts.

He is making clear in this passage that all spiritual gifts come from the triune God—the Father, the Son, and the Spirit. This is clear from 1 Corinthians 12:4-7, as well as from verses 24-28.

It is important to establish the distinction between ministry gifts and manifestation gifts. Many who are writing and teaching on the subject of spiritual gifts make no distinction between these two kinds of spiritual gifts. This causes confusion among many classical pentecostals, who have been teaching on the "gifts of the Spirit" for three-quarters of a century. But they have been thinking only of the manifestations listed in 1 Corinthians 12. It is good that the church is now studying spiritual gifts from the broader perspective, but it is not good to confuse the distinctions between these two.

CHARACTERISTICS OF MINISTRY GIFTS

There are five characteristics of ministry gifts that need to be etched in our minds.

(1) Ministry gifts are permanent. Each believer is given a gift, or a gift-mix, to equip him to minister in the body of Christ. These endowments become permanently a part of his spiritual life. Every Christian needs to identify and develop those gifts.

(2) Ministry gifts usually are related to natural gifts. That does not mean that they are natural gifts. But it does mean that they are in harmony with natural abilities and talents. For example, a ministry of music will be given to one who has some natural musical tendencies. The Holy Spirit lifts out some of the natural gifts and accentuates and adds His supernatural power to them in order to enable one to function powerfully in the church.

(3) Ministry gifts determine the position of an individual in the body of Christ. If an individual has the gift of teaching, he ought to be a teacher. If a person has the gift of pastor-teacher, he ought to be pastoring.

(4) Ministry gifts have to do with persons. In a sense, ministry gifts are gifted persons. The gifts become the possession of those persons, and those persons are then given to the church. That is why it is so important that we learn to accept people and their gifts. We must accept the person in order to receive the ministry he gives.

(5) Each believer must identify and develop his own ministry gifts. All believers have been given ministry gifts, but many have not yet opened the gift, which remains largely undiscovered and thus undeveloped.

CHARACTERISTICS OF MANIFESTATION GIFTS

Just as with ministry gifts, manifestation gifts have five characteristics.

(1) Manifestation gifts are temporary. They are not given to individuals on a permanent basis. In the Scripture there is no such thing as a ministry of tongues. There are manifestations of tongues, but not a ministry of tongues. No individual permanently receives any of these manifestation gifts. They are the surprises of the Spirit—those spontaneous outshinings of the presence of the Spirit in the church. Once they have been manifested, they no longer are in the possession of the individual, though they may be manifested repeatedly through that individual.

(2) Manifestation gifts have no relation to natural ability. Often the person used in a manifestation of the Spirit is the most unlikely person in the congregation. A person who would never preach a sermon in his life may give a prophetic utterance. It may be wise to point out here that there is only one gift that is both a ministry gift and a manifestation gift. That is the gift of prophecy. We will discuss that more in a later chapter.

(3) There is little relationship between a person's position in the body of Christ and the manifestation gifts. They may be given through any member of the Body. Certain of the manifestation gifts are more likely to be given through the leadership of the church for reasons which we will discuss later.

(4) In manifestation gifts, the gift is emphasized and not the person. It is dangerous for a person who has been used in a manifestation of the Spirit to be considered the source of that manifestation. Disaster and tragedy can come to a church when a person is put on a pedestal because he has been used in a supernatural manifestation. These are manifestations of the *Spirit,* not the manifestation of the gift of the individual. These manifestations of the Spirit are not resident in the individual, but in the Holy Spirit. Once the manifestation is finished, the person being used is no longer in possession of the manifestation.

(5) The body of Christ is to receive and rejoice in these surprises of the Spirit. Both ministry gifts and manifestation gifts are essential to a healthy New Testament church. No church can grow and develop as it should and be everything God intends it to be, if it does not have the permanent ministry gifts being continually discovered and developed. But at the same time, there also must be present those surprises of the Spirit—the manifestations of His supernatural activity revealing His presence.

Let us conclude this chapter by reviewing some of the principles we have found.

First there are differences in gifts. There is one church. There is one Spirit. But there are many members, and there are many gifts—not only many gifts, but several categories of gifts. There are leadership gifts, body ministry gifts, and manifestation gifts. We must distinguish between these three categories.

Second, we must identify and develop our ministry gifts. The equipping of the church should involve this process.

Third, we must learn to be receptive and sensitive to the manifestations of the Spirit. The healthy New Testament church must both receive and rejoice in the manifestations of the Spirit.

STUDY QUESTIONS FOR CHAPTER 1

1. What four passages of Scripture provide the basis for our study of spiritual gifts?

2. Define the difference between ministry gifts and manifestation gifts.

3. Name the four equipping ministry gifts.

4. Why do we call manifestation gifts the "surprises of the Spirit"?

CHAPTER TWO

———— ◆ ————

Equipping Ministry Gifts

A ny clear understanding of the subject of spiritual gifts must include a thorough examination of the equipping ministry gifts in the church. This study will focus on Ephesians 4:11-16.

> It was he who gave some to be apostles, some to be prophets, some to be evangelists, and some to be pastors and teachers, to prepare God's people for works of service, so that the body of Christ may be built up until we all reach unity in the faith and in the knowledge of the Son of God and become mature, attaining to the whole measure of the fullness of Christ. Then we will no longer be infants, tossed back and forth by the waves, and blown here and there by every wind of teaching and by the cunning and craftiness of men in their deceitful scheming. Instead, speaking the truth in love, we will in all things grow up into him who is the Head, that is, Christ. From him the whole body, joined and held together by every supporting ligament grows and builds itself up in love, as each part does its work (NIV).

Christ has given to His church certain people to provide leadership. These persons are given equipping ministry gifts. The primary task of these leaders is to equip the church for her ministry, which is the building of the church.

WHO ARE THE EQUIPPERS

There are four equipping ministry gifts: apostle, prophet, evangelist, and pastor-teacher. I am listing pastor-teacher as one office. Teaching is also listed as one of the body ministry gifts. But the grammatical construction here indicates that "pastors and teachers" refers to one office, not two different offices. And so we are listing them as four: the apostle, the prophet, the evangelist, and the pastor-teacher.

The occurrence of these four terms in the New Testament is most interesting. The word *prophet* occurs 149 times. The word *apostle* occurs 79 times. The word *evangelist* occurs only three times in the entire New Testament. The word *pastor* is found only in this passage in the New Testament. However, we must remember that there are other synonyms for pastor. Such words as *elder, bishop,* and *shepherd* refer to the same equipping ministry.

Let us examine briefly the equipping ministry gifts.

(1) Apostle.

There are three levels of apostleship found in the New Testament. Much misunderstanding and controversy can be avoided by distinguishing between these three levels of apostleship.

First, the Lord Jesus Christ is an apostle. Hebrews 3:1 tells us that Jesus Christ is "the Apostle and High Priest of our profession." He is the one and only apostle who is the perfect messenger of God, the One sent forth from the Father, the only One who perfectly reveals the will of the Father. That is a unique and distinct category of apostleship.

Second, there are the twelve men whom Christ sent forth and called apostles. Luke 6:13 tells us that "he chose twelve, whom also he named apostles." He then lists them in verses 14-16. Judas fell from his apostleship and was replaced by Matthias (Acts 1:15-26). There were special requirements for these twelve men (vv. 21, 22), and they hold a special place in the history of the church. These twelve form a unique and unrepeatable level of apostleship.

But the New Testament gives another category of apostles which we must not overlook. Others were called apostles who were not among the Twelve. Paul calls himself "the apostle to the Gentiles." In fact, the word *apostle* is used more frequently for the apostle Paul than for any of the others. He was appointed of the Lord as an apostle to the Gentiles.

There are those who teach that Paul really was God's choice to replace Judas and that the church made a mistake in electing Matthias. But the New Testament nowhere criticizes the choice of Matthias, and it may be somewhat presumptuous for us to do so. Even if this teaching were true, it would not alter the fact that others are called apostles in the New Testament.

James, the Lord's brother, is called an apostle (Galatians 1:19). Barnabas is called an apostle (Acts 14:4, 14). In Romans 16:7 Andronicus and Junias are named as "among the apostles." In 1 Corinthians 15:5–7 Paul lists the appearance of Jesus after His resurrection. He says in verse 5 that He was seen of the Twelve. Then in verse 7 he writes, "After that, he was seen of James; then of **all the apostles**"* Who were these *other* "apostles"? Evidently, James the Lord's brother and others were considered apostles in addition to the Twelve. This third level of apostleship continues to this day in the church.

What is the ministry of the apostle? An apostle is a person with the special ability to provide authoritative leadership for a cluster of churches. This often involves the founding of the churches but may also include giving new direction to the church. The apostle then is a pioneer. Pioneer missionaries are prime examples of apostles in our day. Some would say that an apostle is one who has all the other leadership gifts. He would thus be a prophet, an evangelist, and a pastor-teacher. The apostle then is the unique leader who either plants the church or gives new direction to the church. He is a change agent if he is in a church that is already established.

(2) Prophet.

The prophet is the man with the supernatural ability to interpret the Scriptures in the light of the present situation

*Emphasis mine

in the church. His ministry is to correct, encourage, and edify. The prophetic ministry often involves correcting the church and bringing her back to her primary nature and purpose.

Throughout the history of the church, God has given her many prophets. The church cannot survive without the prophetic voice. The tendency to drift and to lose certain vital emphases makes it absolutely necessary that there be prophets to speak the Word of God to His church in every age. And so this prophetic ministry is essential to the health and well-being of the church in every generation.

(3) Evangelist.

The evangelist is gifted by the Holy Spirit with the unique ability to present the gospel in such a winsome and powerful way that people will respond to the claims of the Lord Jesus Christ through repentance, conversion and discipleship. But not only does he have the ability to evangelize, he also has the ability to equip the church to evangelize. There are those given to the church as evangelists, whose primary responsibility is to lead the church in evangelism and to equip the saints for their work in evangelizing. This tremendously important equipping ministry is essential for the growth and expansion of the church.

(4) Pastor-Teacher.

Some make "pastors and teachers" two offices and thus teach a fivefold equipping ministry. But the evidence seems rather heavy in favor of making this one office. Kenneth Wuest says, "The words 'pastors' and 'teachers' are in a construction called Granvill Sharp's rule which indicates that they refer to one individual" (*Word Studies In The New Testament—Ephesians,* Scripture Truth, p. 101). William Barclay comments, "It would seem that this double phrase describes one set of people" (*Daily Study Bible, Letters To The Galatians And Ephesians,* Westminster, p. 174). H. C. G. Moule says that these two words are "two sides of one work; men who were set over the local 'flocks' of believers to be their leaders and instructors in the Lord" (*Ephesian Studies,* Zondervan, p. 191).

The previous three equipping ministry gifts seem to have

been itinerant ministries in the early church. But here is a gift that belongs to the local church—the pastor-teacher. It is the special ability to take responsibility for the nourishment, health, protection, and development of a congregation on a relatively long-term basis.

The pastor-teacher is the one who takes the responsibility for shepherding the flock. He makes a commitment to a congregation for as long as God wills, often for a lifetime.

WHAT IS THE EQUIPPING MINISTRY?

What is the work of these men with equipping ministry gifts? Ephesians 4:12 tells us: "For the perfecting of the saints." The word *perfecting* (*katartisman* in the Greek) can be translated by several English words. The Greek verb *katartidzo* means to mend, to restore, to set right, to make complete, to strive for perfection.

A key to the ministry of equipping may be found in the use of the Greek word *katartidzo* (and its derivatives) in the New Testament. From this key we may define the eightfold ministry of these equippers. This ministry may be described by eight words: *mending, organizing, restoring, equipping, training, maturing, uniting,* and *perfecting.*

(1) Mending.

In Matthew 4:21 we read: "And going on from thence, he saw other two brethren, James the son of Zebedee, and John his brother, in a ship with Zebedee their father, **mending their nets**;* and he called them." The word translated "mending" is the same word used in Ephesians 4:12 that is translated "perfecting." These fishermen were repairing their nets in preparation for fishing. Nets were tools of their trade. Without good nets they would be wasting their time fishing. It was imperative that they mend their broken nets.

Jesus promised His disciples that they would become fishers of men. This focuses on the ministry of evangelism. The church is God's evangelistic instrument on earth. The equippers of the church must therefore mend nets in order to make

*Emphasis mine

the fishers of men more effective. In other words, the leaders in the church must prepare the church for her work of evangelism.

(2) Organizing.

In Hebrews 11:3 we read: "Through faith we understand that the worlds were **framed*** by the word of God...." The New England Bible (NEB) renders this word "fashioned." The basic idea is to organize. God so organized (framed) the universe that all things work together according to what we call "natural law." Man can pinpoint with absolute accuracy where the various stars and planets were at any given time in history. This is possible only because of God's carefully organized creation.

The church also must be organized. Each member should know his place and function in the body of Christ. The God-given leaders must help each member of the Body find his place. This means that he must discover and develop his spiritual gifts, but he must also find his position in the Body. Some people have held to the idea that organization is unspiritual. This is certainly not the teaching of Scripture. God is the greatest organizer of all, and as His children we must be like Him. It is the task of the **equipping ministry** to **organize** the church.

(3) Restoring.

In Galatians 6:1 we read: "Brethren, if a man be overtaken in a fault, ye which are spiritual, **restore*** such an one in the spirit of meekness; considering thyself, lest thou also be tempted." The NIV reads: "Brothers, if someone is caught in a sin, you who are spiritual should **restore*** him gently. But watch yourself, or you also may be tempted." The NEB renders this word "set him right."

This passage deals specifically with the responsibility for bringing wayward saints back into the fold. The mark of spirituality is to engage in the restoring ministry. Those who are overtaken or trapped by sin are to be restored to the fellowship of the church. This ministry of restoration is essential in a healthy church. It is part of the task of the equippers.

*Emphasis mine

(4) Equipping.

This is the basic word which we will use primarily in describing the ministry of those in leadership in the church. In Hebrews 13:20, 21 we read: "Now the God of peace, that brought again from the dead our Lord Jesus, that great shepherd of the sheep, through the blood of the everlasting covenant, Make you **perfect in every good work*** to do his will, working in you that which is well-pleasing in his sight, through Jesus Christ; to whom be glory for ever and ever. Amen." The NIV reads, "equip you with everything good for doing his will...." This prayer of benediction calls attention to God's purposes to equip His people for their work of ministry. It again directs our thoughts to the work of the leadership ministry gifts. These individuals are to **equip the saints for their work of ministry.**

The only test of the effectiveness of the equippers is the effectiveness of those whom they are equipping. How well is the church doing in its ministry? This is the gauge for measuring the performance of the leaders. It is not how well the leaders perform in public, but how well the church performs in her ministry to the Lord, to the fellowship of believers, and to the world of lost men.

(5) Training.

In Luke 6:40 we read: "The disciple is not above his master: but every one that is **perfect*** shall be as his master." The NIV reads: "A student is not above his teacher, but everyone who is **fully trained*** will be like his teacher." The idea is the educating of a student, the training of a pupil.

Training is essential for most work a person will do. Christian ministry is no exception. In fact, it is more important in this realm than in any other. No person can serve the church effectively without training. He must develop his ministry. He must work faithfully under others before he is able to lead effectively himself. The church then is a training ground. Some would make the church a parade ground for the performance of the leaders, but the biblical view is that the church is a training ground for the preparation of the

*Emphasis mine

25

saints for their work of ministry.

(6) Maturing.

In 1 Peter 5:10 we read: "And after you have suffered for a little while, the God of all grace, who called you to His eternal glory in Christ, will Himself **perfect**,* confirm, strengthen and establish you" (New American Standard Bible, NASB). Phillips translates this word "make you whole."

This perfecting, or maturing, of the saints takes time. A child born into a home is as much a member of that family as he will ever be. Likewise, a person who has been born-again is just as much a member of God's family as he will ever be. But it is also true that a baby must grow and mature before he can join his father in running the family business. In the same way, a born-again believer must grow and mature before becoming a full-grown participant in the work of the church.

Thus the **maturing of believers** is just as important as the **multiplying of believers.** This is the work of the leadership ministry in the church. So the leadership of the church must be concerned with the growth and development of the believers committed to their care.

(7) Uniting.

In 1 Corinthians 1:10 we read: "Now I beseech you, brethren, by the name of our Lord Jesus Christ, that ye all speak the same thing, and that there be no divisions among you; but that ye be **perfectly joined together*** in the same mind and in the same judgment." Here again is the word *katartidzo (katartis-menoi),* translated "perfecting" in Ephesians 4:12. Here the word refers to perfecting the unity which belongs to the people of God. The NIV reads "perfectly united." Weymouth gives "perfect harmony." We will come later in our study to the problem of harmonizing spiritual gifts, but this passage indicates that part of the ministry of equipping the saints is the ministry of uniting. In Ephesians 4:3 Paul urges that the walk of the believers includes "endeavoring to keep the **unity in the Spirit*** in the bond of peace." The equippers are to bring this unity to perfection.

*Emphasis mine

(8) Perfecting.

This is the word used in Ephesians 4:12. In Matthew 21:16 we have a beautiful use of this word: "And Jesus saith unto them, Yea; have ye never read, Out of the mouth of babes and sucklings thou **hast perfected praise**?"* The NIV reads, "From the lips of children and infants you **have ordained praise.**"* It is significant that this word is used in this passage! The perfecting of the saints must include the perfecting of praise in God's people. Or, maybe it would be better to say **raise up praise** in the church. Praising God is one of the great occupations of those who serve Him. May He perfect His church in this ministry of praise.

These eight words give us a rather complete picture of the work of apostles, prophets, evangelists, and pastor-teachers.

WHAT IS THE MINISTRY OF THE CHURCH?

Looking again at Ephesians 4:16 we want to focus on the phrase "fitly joined together." We will call that "mutuality." Also note the phrase "the effectual working in the measure of every part." Each member of the church is to minister to each of the other members of the church. The equipping ministry of the church is meant to develop this mutuality, this shared life, this ministry of each member to the Body. How we need to understand that the Christian religion is based upon an unusual relationship between people. The church is people, but it is always people together in a community of loving relationships. It is never people in isolation.

Jesus gave the simplest definition of the church when He said, "For where two or three are gathered together in my name, there am I in the midst of them" (Matthew 18:20).

What is the church? This can be answered with five statements. First, the church is people. Second, the church is people together (in community). Third, the church is people together loving God (worshiping). Fourth, the church is people together loving one another (sharing the life of Christ). Fifth, the church is people together loving the

*Emphasis mine

27

world (evangelizing).

The equipping ministry gifts are given to the church to equip her to be this community of worshiping, loving, witnessing sons of God. This alone will make her fit to carry on the ministry of Jesus Christ in a hostile, hurting world. Each member of the body of Christ is to minister to the Body with the gifts God has given to him. The equipper must therefore help each member discover and develop his spiritual gifts, as well as to join the members properly in a way that will maximize this mutual ministry.

Finally, note that this is all to he done "in love." In Ephesians 4:2 we are told that our ministry involves "forbearing one another in love." That means putting up with one another in love. We must be tolerant of one another, knowing that God has not finished with any of us yet. We are still "human beings." We are being made into His image, but not finished yet. Then in verse 16 we read, "the edifying of itself in love." The building of the church is done only in love. The growth of the body of Christ is possible only in the atmosphere of love. In fact, loving God, loving one another, and loving the world (as God so loved the world) are the three chief activities of the church.

STUDY QUESTIONS FOR CHAPTER 2

1. What are the three levels of apostleship?

2. List the eight words that define the eightfold ministry of equipping.

3. What is the church? Define it in five statements.

4. What are the saints being equipped to do?

CHAPTER THREE

The Fourfold Task of the Shepherd

The gift of pastor-teacher is the most prevalent of the equipping ministry gifts. The other three were largely itinerant ministries in the early church, but it seems that each local church had several pastor-teachers, often called elders.

Every church needs a pastor-teacher. No church is planted until elders (or pastors) are ordained to lead the flock. In reaction to the false distinction between clergy and laity, some in our day have decided to reject the whole idea of pastoral leadership. They would opt for a church without a shepherd. This is both unscriptural and, in the long run, unworkable. Christ is pictured in the first chapter of the book of Revelation as holding the pastors ("stars") of the churches in His right hand. The "angels" of the churches are the pastor-teachers. They are God's gifts to the churches.

Since the gift of pastor-teacher is so important, let us examine this gift a little more in detail. Remember the definition that we gave in the last chapter: "The pastor-teacher has the special ability to take responsibility for the nourishment, health, protection, and development of a congregation on a relatively long-term basis."

Someone has observed that the evangelist is like an obstetrician. He has to do with the birth of babes in Christ. The pastor-teacher is the pediatrician. He has to do with the growth and health of these babes.

We want to look more closely at the task of these God-given shepherds. In Acts 20:28-30 we find some counsel given by the apostle Paul to the pastors of the church at Ephesus. In the New Testament no reference is made to any church having only one pastor, instead a plurality of pastors served in the churches. The reference to the "angels" of the churches found in Revelation, chapters 1-3, seems to indicate that each church had a head pastor. This does not alter the basic New Testament pattern. Paul said:

> [Guard] yourselves and all the flock of which the Holy Spirit has made you overseers. Be shepherds of the church of God, which he bought with his own blood. I know that after I leave, savage wolves will come in among you and will not spare the flock. Even from your own number men will arise and distort the truth in order to draw away disciples after them (Acts 20:28-30, NIV).

The apostle Peter also offers some advice for pastors. He, too, uses the term *elders.* The word *elder* is used more in the New Testament than is the word *pastor.* But, as we have already noted, the terms *pastor, bishop,* and *elder* all refer to pastor-teachers. Peter writes:

> To the elders among you, I appeal as a fellow elder, a witness of Christ's sufferings and one who also will share in the glory to be revealed: Be shepherds of God's flock that is under your care, serving as over-seers—not because you must, but because you are willing, as God wants you to be; not greedy for money, but eager to serve; not lording it over those entrusted to you, but being examples to the flock. And when the Chief Shepherd appears, you will receive the crown of glory that will never fade away (1 Peter 5:1-4, NIV).

These two passages of Scripture give some tremendous counsel to pastor-teachers. Coming from the two chief apostles of the New Testament church—the apostle to the Jews and the apostle to the Gentiles—these two passages describe the work of the pastor-teacher.

Four words describe the work of a pastor-teacher: *provider,* *pioneer, protector,* and *physician.*

PROVIDER

Remember the language of Jesus to Simon Peter on the banks of the Galilee after He had restored him to his place in fellowship with the apostolic band (John 21:15-17). He was renewing His commission to him. He said, "Simon, do you love me?" and Simon Peter answered, "Surely I love you!" Jesus said, "Feed my sheep." Twice He emphasized the task of feeding the sheep. (In the second command Jesus used the word for *shepherd,* rather than *feed.*)

The pastor-teacher is to be a provider. He is to feed the people the Bread and the Water of life, the milk and the meat of the Word, even the strong meat of the Word. If he is going to feed the flock, he must be a diligent student of the Scriptures. It is sad to see a flock of God's sheep hungry and undernourished. Many churches are weak and ineffective for the simple reason that the shepherd has not fed the sheep. There has been no true pastor to provide nourishment.

Of course, sometimes there are spoiled sheep who want a diet of candy and ice cream. And when the pastor gives them meat, they complain that they haven't been fed. Others are not interested in the sincere milk of the Word or the Bread of life. They want only some kind of exotic delicacy. But sometimes the sheep are fed nothing of substance because the shepherd is ill prepared to feed them.

The pastor-teacher must know how to feed the Word of God to the people of God. In order to do this he must know the Bible. The equipping of the saints is contingent upon a pastor-teacher who is well versed in the Bible. He must be continually a student of the Word. If he ever stops studying and expanding his knowledge of the Word, he will become stagnant and ineffective in his ministry.

A person may have a fruitful ministry for years. His congregation may grow and prosper. But if he settles into a spiritual rut and stops developing his ministry, it gradually will lose its effectiveness. He may excuse himself by saying that people no longer respond to the truth as they once did, but in reality the problem is that his ministry has become stale and tasteless. Feeding the flock demands continual preparation by the shepherd. He must maintain a freshness in his ministry of the Word. Stale bread does not appeal to people.

If the shepherd is to be a provider and feed the sheep, he himself must feed on the Word of God. Nothing will take the place of that. He must also know how to prepare the food that he feeds the people. It is not enough to be a student of the Bible, to feed himself by Bible study, he also must know how to communicate the Word to the people.

Some shepherds feel that it is not important to study psychology, methods of teaching or homiletics. They know the truth, but have little ability to communicate it to others. They fail to feed the flock, even though they have great knowledge of the truth. The process of communication has eluded them.

The pastor-teacher should prepare his spiritual meal for his flock just as carefully as a good cook prepares a natural meal. The same truth can be presented in an attractive and appealing manner or in a distasteful manner.

PIONEER

It is crucial to understand that one does not drive sheep; he leads them. The shepherd must walk ahead of the sheep and show them the way. The apostle Paul had the right approach when he said, "Be ye followers of me, even as I also am of Christ" (1 Corinthians 11:1).

It is important for the pastor-teacher to be a pioneer, a file leader for the members of the congregation. If he wants a praying church, he must be a praying pastor. Sermons on prayer are a poor substitute for the pastor who is a role model. A pastor who can say, "Follow me in a life of prayer," is doing what Jesus did. It was His prayer life that triggered His disciples to say, "Lord, teach us how to pray." Why did the disciples make this request? It was because they had watched Him praying. They had heard Him praying. As they watched Him pray, they could see how much they needed to learn to pray. All the sermons on prayer that one can preach will not bring such a response.

The shepherd also must be a leader, a pioneer, in Bible study. Many Christians neglect to study the Bible, and there are several reasons for that neglect. One of the most important reasons is that they have had no example. The pastor-teacher has not been a role model. Bible study is something that one learns to do. Because a person has been born again does not mean he automatically knows how to study the Bible.

The pastor-teacher also must lead in witnessing. It is sadly ineffective to tell Christians to go out into the world and witness if there is no pastoral leadership showing the way. The leader of one of the great lay witnessing ministries in the United States once indicated that his best students were pastors—as long as the studying was in the classroom. But when they moved from the classroom out into the streets, these same pastors became his most frightened and ineffective students. It seems the pastors were great on theory, but weak on practice. This may indicate the major hindrance to developing witnessing churches. Pastoral leadership is essential in the area of witnessing. Every dynamic, evangelistic church must have a dynamic, evangelistic pastoral leader, someone to show the people how to communicate the gospel. This may require the presence of a team member with the gift of evangelist.

The pastor also must lead the way in the grace of giving. There is only one way for a pastor to be good at receiving offerings. He must be good at giving offerings. If a pastor wants his people to give, he must give. When he challenges every family in the church to make a monthly faith commitment for world missions, he must lead the way by making such a commitment himself. There is no better way to raise the level of giving in a church than for the pastor to raise his level of giving. A cheerful, liberal giver in the pulpit will tend to have cheerful, liberal givers in the pew.

He must lead his people in loving one another. This is the chief mark of Christ's people—they love one another (John

13:34). It is essential that the shepherd love the sheep so that the sheep will learn by his example how to love one another. We are not to love in word, the Bible tells us, but in deed and in truth (1 John 3:18). The pastor-teacher must be a pioneer in showing people what loving relationships are all about.

PROTECTOR

So the pastor-teacher is a provider and a pioneer. But he also must be a protector. The Bible teaches us that a shepherd will give his life defending his sheep. A part of the equipment which the shepherd carried with him was a weapon to fend off the enemies who would attack his sheep. He needed to learn to protect those who were under his care. Paul's counsel to the Ephesian elders makes this responsibility clear. He wrote:

> Take heed therefore unto yourselves, and to all the flock, over the which the Holy Ghost hath made you overseers, to feed the church of God, which he hath purchased with his own blood. For I know this, that after my departing shall grievous wolves enter in among you, not sparing the flock. Also of your own selves shall men arise, speaking perverse things, to draw away disciples after them. Therefore watch, and remember, that by the space of three years I ceased not to warn every one night and day with tears (Acts 20:28-31).

The pastor must be vigilant. He must know the enemy. He must be mindful of the dangers that lurk about his flock. He must be willing to defend his flock with his life.

Jesus said, "I am the good shepherd: the good shepherd giveth his life for the sheep. But he that is an hireling, and not the shepherd, whose own the sheep are not, seeth the wolf coming, and leaveth the sheep, and fleeth: and the wolf catcheth them, and scattereth the sheep. The hireling fleeth, because he is an hireling, and careth not for the sheep" (John 10:11-13).

PHYSICIAN

Finally, the pastor-teacher is a healer of the sheep. He must know the signs of spiritual health and the symptoms of spiritual diseases.

There are two kinds of healing in the church. First, there is individual healing. The shepherd is concerned about the personal health of each member of the flock. He yearns to present each one to the Great Shepherd in a state of soundness and health—spirit, soul, and body.

Second, there is a healing of relationships. The health of the church depends on healthy interpersonal relationships. It is important that the pastor know how to heal joints that connect the members of the church, when these joints are not functioning properly. So the pastor is concerned about the health of each member of the Body, but he is also concerned about the health of the Body as a whole. The shepherd's concern is for the whole person as well as the whole body of Christ.

Each individual in the Body is spirit, soul, and body. First, he is a spirit. *Pneuma* is the Greek word which refers to man's God-consciousness. This is the part of man that especially relates to God, who is a spirit. The pastor, first of all, needs to know how to minister healing to the spirit.

Man also is a soul (*psuche* in the Greek). This is man's self-consciousness. This includes man's intellect and emotions. It also includes his self-esteem. A believer's concept of himself may need healing. Sin destroys man's perception of his own ultimate worth to God. It blinds him to the fact that he is the object of God's infinite love. Even after entering into the fellowship of believers, many fall far short of accepting themselves as the apple of God's eye. The Holy Spirit has to bring healing to a warped and twisted self-image. A wholesome Christian attitude demands a ministry of healing to the memories and to the mental habits of the new believer.

There is also a ministry to the Body, the *soma*. The body is the instrument of expression for the soul and the spirit of man. The pastor-teacher ministers healing to the spirit, the soul, and the body. Four characteristics of a wholesome

Christian, one who has been made whole in spirit, soul, and body are found in 1 Thessalonians 5:16-24.

First, he has an optimistic attitude. In verses 16-18 the believer is described as praying without ceasing and giving thanks in everything. He has a good attitude.

Second, there is a keen sensitivity to the Spirit. In verses 19 and 20, the believer is described as one who neither quenches the fire of the Spirit nor despises prophetic utterances. Rather, he tests the spiritual manifestations and holds on to that which is good and profitable.

Third, he has a balanced personality. The spirit, soul and body are preserved blameless unto the coming of the Lord. The Lord is coming for a people who have been made whole, people who belong to God, spiritually, mentally, and physically.

Finally, there is a dependence upon God's faithfulness. Paul said, "Faithful is he who hath called you who also will do it" (v. 24). This is the true basis of wholeness. It is not based upon man's faithfulness. Our health is dependent upon *His* faithfulness.

God gives us pastor-teachers who will be providers, pioneers, protectors, and physicians to the flock of God. These God-given shepherds will produce healthy churches full of members who have been made truly whole.

STUDY QUESTIONS FOR CHAPTER 3

1. What other titles are used in the New Testament for pastor-teacher?

2. What is the fourfold task of the pastor?

3. What two kinds of healing are needed in the church?

4. What are the three parts of man's nature?

CHAPTER FOUR

Body Ministry Gifts

The second category of ministry gifts is what we will call *body ministry gifts*. Romans 12:3-8 reads:

> For by the grace given to me I say to every one of you: Do not think of yourself more highly than you ought, but rather think of yourself with sober judgment, in accordance with the measure of faith God has given you. Just as each of us has one body with many members, and these members do not all have the same function, so in Christ we who are many form one body, and each member belongs to all the others. We have different gifts, according to the grace given us. If a man's gift is prophesying, let him use it in proportion to his faith. If it is serving, let him serve; if it is teaching, let him teach; if it is encouraging, let him encourage; if it is contributing to the needs of others, let him give generously; if it is leadership, let him govern diligently; if it is showing mercy, let him do it cheerfully (NIV).

1 Corinthians 12:12-27 gives us the biblical framework for a study of body ministry gifts:

> The body is a unit, though it is made up of many parts; and though all its parts are many, they form one body. So it is with Christ. For we were all baptized

by one Spirit into one body—whether Jews or Greeks, slave or free—and we were all given the one Spirit to drink. Now the body is not made up of one part but of many. If the foot should say, "Because I am not a hand, I do not belong to the body," it would not for that reason cease to be part of the body. And if the ear should say, "Because I am not an eye, I do not belong to the body," it would not for that reason cease to be part of the body. If the whole body were an eye, where would the sense of hearing be? If the whole body were an ear, where would the sense of smell be? But in fact God has arranged the parts in the body, every one of them, just as he wanted them to be. If they were all one part, where would the body be? As it is, there are many parts, but one body.

The eye cannot say to the hand, "I don't need you!" And the head cannot say to the feet, "I don't need you!" On the contrary, those parts of the body that seem to be weaker are indispensable, and the parts that we think are less honorable we treat with special honor. And the parts that are unpresentable are treated with special modesty, while our presentable parts need no special treatment. But God has combined the members of the body and has given greater honor to the parts that lacked it, so that there should be no division in the body, but that its parts should have equal concern for each other. If one part suffers, every part suffers with it; if one part is honored, every part rejoices with it. Now, you are the body of Christ, and each one of you is a part of it (NIV).

DIVERSITY IN UNITY

Two words stand out in these passages: *one* and *many*. *One* body and *many* parts. *One* church, *many* members. *One* purpose, but *many* functions. It is important to recognize the unity of the church. It is also important to be aware of the diversity of the members.

Ephesians 4:1-7 focuses on the unity of the church—*one*

church, *one* Christ, *one* Father, *one* Holy Spirit, *one* faith, *one* hope, *one* baptism. The unity of the church is clearly etched in the New Testament; but we must remember that this is unity in diversity. While the unity is real and essential to the health and well-being of the church, diversity in the members is just as real and just as essential.

God does not make duplicates. All His people are originals. Every member of the body of Christ is unique. His ministry, his gifts, his position in the body of Christ make him unique, different from any other member of the Body.

Since no two individuals have the same combination of spiritual gifts, it is essential that each person discover and develop his own gifts. It is fatal to try to duplicate the ministry of another person. This is not only futile, it is also certain to blind one to his true ministry goal. Each one has been given his own unique place to fill in the church. This requires individual development.

One person may have only one spiritual gift, while another may have a mix of several gifts. The person with one gift may have a highly developed ministry which provides some vital contribution to the life and growth of the church. The gift-mix of another may mean that he has no gift as highly developed as the first person. But he has a much more varied ministry to the body of Christ.

But in each person these gifts are given to equip the member to minister to the Body. Body ministry gifts are to be developed and deployed under the equipping ministry gifts. There is no more important facet of the equipping ministry than the discovering, developing, and deploying of the spiritual gifts resident in the members of the body of Christ. For this reason it is necessary for equippers to have a good grasp of the nature and characteristics of the various body ministry gifts. For our study we will define seven of these gifts.

BODY MINISTRY GIFTS

(1) Exhortation.

Exhortation is the special, supernatural ability to minister encouragement, strength, and hope to other members of the body of Christ. Barnabas was called the Son of Encouragement (Acts 4:36, NIV). The noun form of this word is used for the Holy Spirit (John 14:16, 17, 26). It is also used for Jesus Christ (1 John 2:1). Leslie Flynn describes the gift of exhortation as the ability "to strengthen the weak, reassure the wavering, buttress the buffeted, steady the faltering, console the troubled, encourage the halting" (*19 Gifts of the Spirit,* pp. 82, 83).

(2) Teaching.

This gift of teaching is different from the equipping gift of pastor-teacher. The teacher has the "supernatural ability to explain clearly and apply effectively the truth of the Word of God" (Leslie Flynn). Peter Wagner says that the teacher has the ability "to communicate information relevant to the health and ministry of the body and its members in such a way that others will learn" (*Your Spiritual Gifts Can Help Your Church Grow*, pp. 259, 260).

(3) Service.

The gift of service, or helps, is the supernatural ability to serve the body of Christ in a supporting role, thus releasing other workers (especially those in leadership roles) to carry on their ministries. The best biblical example of the gift of service is found in Acts 6. Seven men were chosen to exercise this gift in the early church, so that the apostles would not be distracted from their equipping ministry. John Mark was also called to this role of "helper" (Acts 13:5). The gift of helps, or service, is a vital part of any dynamic church.

(4) Hospitality.

Hospitality is the God-given ability to provide food and lodging to those in need of it in such a way as to make them feel at home, to feel truly welcome.

Karen Mains, in *Open Heart—Open Home,* states that true hospitality is different from entertaining. Entertaining demands perfection and seeks to impress others with possessions, culinary skills, and social graces. Entertaining puts the emphasis on things rather than people. Everything must be in perfect order before guests are invited.

Scriptural hospitality seeks to minister. It recognizes that home and possessions are gifts from God to be used in His service. Hospitality does not seek to impress, but to serve. It says, "What God has given to me, I gladly share with you." It reaches out to others with no thought of return invitations, but takes pleasure in the joy of giving, doing, loving, and serving.

(5) Administration.

Peter Wagner says the gift of administration, or government, is "the special ability that God gives to certain members of the body of Christ to understand clearly the immediate and long-range goals of a particular unit of the body of Christ and to devise and execute effective plans for the accomplishment of these goals." William McCrae defines it this way: "In extra-Biblical Greek this was the word used for piloting a ship, steering it safely through the rocks to port. This person is able to give vision and direction. He is able to organize and direct toward a specific goal. He sees that everything is done decently and in order. Projects are done in a way that promotes the work of God and the growth of those involved" (*The Dynamics of Spiritual Gifts,* p. 52).

(6) Benevolence.

Leslie Flynn says the gift of benevolence, or mercy, is "the ability to manifest practical, compassionate, cheerful love toward suffering members of the body of Christ." Peter Wagner says it is "to feel genuine empathy and compassion for individuals, both Christian and non-Christian, who suffer distressing physical, mental, or emotional problems, and to translate that compassion into cheerfully done deeds that reflect Christ's love and alleviate the suffering."

(7) Giving.

Finally, the gift of giving is the ability and disposition to provide material resources to the church with joy and liberality. All Christians should do this, but there are those for whom this is a special gift. It is their ministry.

By way of review, let us list again and briefly define these seven gifts.

1. *Exhorter*—one with the special ability to minister encouragement, strength, and hope to other members of the body of Christ.

2. *Teacher*—one with the ability to communicate clearly

and to apply effectively the truth of the Word of God.

3. *Service or Helps*—the ability or aptitude to serve the body of Christ in a supporting role, thus releasing other workers, especially those with leadership gifts, to carry on their ministries.

4. *Hospitality*—the God-given ability to provide a warm welcome, food, and lodging to members of the body of Christ, even to the point of "entertaining strangers" (Hebrews 13:2).

5. *Benevolence*—the ability and the disposition to administer loving and compassionate service to suffering and helpless people, especially to members of the body of Christ.

6. *Giving*—the disposition and capacity to minister material resources to the body of Christ with liberality and cheerfulness.

7. *Administration or governments*—the ability to organize and direct the activities of the church so that she will fulfill her mission.

THE BODY ILLUSTRATION

In Romans 12:3-8 and in 1 Corinthians 12:12-27, the apostle Paul uses the human body to illustrate the functioning of spiritual gifts. There are many members but one body. He uses the eye, the ear, the hand, etc., to illustrate the different ministries given to the various members of the church. As the apostle etches the picture, it becomes obvious how ludicrous it is for any one member to be jealous of another—or even to want to do the ministry of another. Each member has a role to play in the functioning of the Body. This role is determined by the spiritual gifts of that individual.

Just as each cell in a person's body contains the genetic structure of that individual, so each member of the body of Christ contains the imprint of the image of Christ. But at the same time each cell has its own place to fill in the body. There is a unity in the one Body, but there is a beautiful diversity in the individual members of that one Body.

Each person has programmed into every cell of his body, his personal traits like color of eyes, hair, and skin; shape of nose, feet, and ears; and the basic physical and mental characteristics which are uniquely his. These traits become apparent as the child matures into adulthood.

Recently, scientists discovered an amazing capacity in body cells. Cells function according to their location in the body. A liver cell functions far differently from a brain cell, etc. But when cells are transplanted from one part of the body to another, they function according to their new location in the body. A brain cell transplanted to the liver will soon start functioning like a liver cell. It seems that cells are committed to the unity of the body and adapt to serve the body wherever they are.

What a lesson for Christians! The uniqueness of each member of the body of Christ necessitates that each be dealt with according to his gifts and ministry. No two members can be expected to perform in the same way.

That means that pastors cannot find a mold into which they can pour believers. God only knows how many people have been stunted rather than developed, all because of a lack of understanding the concept of spiritual gifts.

The ministry of the church must be determined to a great degree by the gifts found in its members. For example, there should be only as many Sunday School classes as there are people with the gift of teaching. It is counterproductive to have classes taught by people with no gift of teaching. It would be better to have five classes with five teachers than to have twenty classes with five teachers and fifteen "babysitters."

The first step in organizing a congregation of believers should be to discover the spiritual gifts of the members. The teaching ministry of the church should be tailor-made to fit the gift-mix of the congregation. Evangelism is the task of the whole church, and all believers are to be witnesses. But the style of the evangelistic outreach will be determined largely by the spiritual gifts of the pastoral staff and the members.

While shortages of needed personnel should not be allowed to cripple the church permanently, an awareness of the spiritual gifts available should give some guidance in the strategy for growth in the congregation. Don't devise an organization and then force people to fit into the organizational mold. Rather, study the people whom God has put together and then organize around these God-given ministries.

Certain functions are essential in a church—worship, teaching, evangelizing, etc. The form that these activities take in any church should be determined to some extent by the spiritual gifts of the equippers and the people they are equipping.

Thus, it is important to discover all the spiritual gifts in the church and to set about developing these gifts to the maximum. Many (possibly most) churches have a wealth of gifts resident in the members. But in too many cases these gifts have not been developed and deployed.

It is also important to remember that even regarding spiritual gifts, all members are dependent upon the Body. The eye functions as an eye *only* as long as it remains in the body. The moment the eye ceases to be a member of the body, it ceases to function as an eye. The hand operates as a hand only within the context of the body. If the hand is severed from the body, it loses all its remarkable ability as a hand. This is true of every member of the body. Not one is made with the capacity to operate apart from the body.

How beautifully this illustrates the ministry of believers. The ministry operates only when in vital contact with other believers. No ministry can function when cut off from the rest of the body of Christ. The very life of the member is vitally joined to the life of the Body. Spiritual gifts are meant for the Body. The Body is essential to their development and ministry. We must then be intensely concerned about the health and wholeness of the Body.

Let us all be committed to identifying and developing spiritual gifts—not just our own, but those of every member of the church.

STUDY QUESTIONS FOR CHAPTER 4

1. What two words stand out in Paul's description of the church as a "body"?

2. Why must each person in the body of Christ receive special attention?

3. List the seven typical body ministry gifts.

4. What should be the first step in organizing a congregation of believers?

CHAPTER FIVE

Harmonizing
The Gifts

O ne of the chief tasks of the equippers in the church is to harmonize the various spiritual gifts in the members of the body of Christ. Our scriptural basis for this study is Ephesians 4:11-13, 16.

In verses 11-13, Paul writes, "It was he who gave some to be apostles, some to be prophets, some to be evangelists, and some to be pastors and teachers, to prepare God's people for works of service, so that the body of Christ may be built up until we all reach unity in the faith and in the knowledge of the Son of God and become mature, attaining to the whole measure of the fullness of Christ" (NIV).

In verse 16 we read, "From him the whole body, joined and held together by every supporting ligament, grows and builds itself up in love, as each part does its work" (NIV).

In order to understand better the need for harmonizing the gifts, we need to review our list of spiritual gifts. We concluded that there are different kinds of spiritual gifts. Paul says this in 1 Corinthians 12:4. The truth is confirmed by the variety of Greek words used in the New Testament. At least eight different words used in the Greek New Testament are translated by our English word "gift." Other words, such as the Greek word *phanerosis,* also have to do with spiritual gifts. We identified three kinds of spiritual gifts—*equipping ministry gifts, body ministry gifts,* and *manifestation gifts.*

EQUIPPING MINISTRY GIFTS

The Greek word *domata* is used in Ephesians 4:8 to refer to the *equipping ministry gifts*. These leadership gifts are named in verse 11.

(1) Apostle. This is the person with the special ability to provide authoritative leadership for a cluster of churches. This often involves the founding of churches, but may also focus on giving new direction to the churches.

(2) Prophet. This is that gifted person who has the supernatural ability to interpret the Scriptures in light of the present situation in the church. The prophetic gift is correcting, encouraging, and edifying.

(3) Evangelist. An evangelist is that person with the ability to present the gospel in such a way that people will respond to the claims of Christ by repentance, conversion, and discipleship. The evangelist also has the ability to prepare others for this ministry of evangelizing.

(4) Pastor-teacher. This is the person with the special ability to take responsibility for the nourishment, health, protection, and development of a congregation on a relatively long-term basis.

BODY MINISTRY GIFTS

The second category of spiritual gifts is *body ministry gifts*. In chapter 4 are listed seven typical body ministry gifts.

(1) Exhortation—the special ability to minister encouragement, strength, and hope to other members of the body of Christ.

(2) Teaching—the ability to communicate clearly and apply effectively the truth of the Word of God.

(3) Service (or helps)—the aptitude and ability to serve the body of Christ in a supporting role, thus releasing other workers, especially those with leadership gifts, to carry on their ministries.

(4) Administration (or governments)—the ability to organize and direct the activities of the church so that she will fulfill her mission.

(5) Benevolence—the ability and the disposition to minister loving and compassionate service to suffering and helpless members of the body of Christ.

(6) Giving—the disposition and capacity to minister material resources to the body of Christ with liberality and cheerfulness.

(7) Hospitality—the God-given ability to provide a warm welcome, food, and lodging to members of the body of Christ, even to the point of "entertaining strangers" (Hebrews 13:2).

MANIFESTATION GIFTS

The third category is *manifestation gifts*. These are the nine gifts listed in 1 Corinthians 12:8-10: *a word of wisdom, a word of knowledge, faith, gifts of healing, miracles, prophecy, discerning of spirits, tongues, and interpretation of tongues.*

CHARACTERISTICS OF MINISTRY AND MANIFESTATION GIFTS

There are some basic differences between ministry gifts and manifestation gifts. And those responsible for harmonizing the gifts must recognize these differences. We listed five basic characteristics of these two kinds of spiritual gifts.

(1) Ministry gifts are *permanent*. These gifts are given to believers and become a continual part of their life in Christ.

(2) Ministry gifts are *related to natural gifts*. They are not natural abilities, but are generally based upon the innate abilities of the individual.

(3) Ministry gifts *determine the position one holds in the body of Christ.* One's spiritual gift or gifts should be the basis for his ministry in the church.

(4) Ministry gifts are really *gifted persons.* In order for the church to receive the gift(s), she must receive the person.

(5) Each believer is to *identify* and *develop* his ministry gift(s).

Manifestation gifts stand somewhat in contrast to ministry gifts:

(1) They are *temporary.* They are not given permanently to an individual. They are outshinings of the Holy Spirit at a specific time and place. When the manifestation is over, the gift is no longer the possession of the individual.

(2) Manifestation gifts have *no relation to natural ability.* The person used in a manifestation may be the person most unlikely to be used as far as natural ability is concerned.

(3) Manifestation gifts have *little relationship to the position in the body of Christ.* Manifestations do not determine one's ministry in the church. There are, however, certain manifestations which are given more often than not through the leadership in the church.

(4) The *gift is emphasized here,* and not the person. It is a manifestation of the Spirit, and it is this manifestation which must be received. The person being used is just a channel.

(5) The body is to *receive* and *rejoice* in these surprises of the Spirit.

DIRECTOR OF THE SYMPHONY

One of the primary responsibilities of the equipping ministries of the church is to bring all the gifts into harmonious operation in the church. The functioning of spiritual gifts should form a spiritual symphony.

It is important to understand that in the church there are no two people alike. God does not make duplicates. All of God's people—all of the members of the body of Christ—are originals. This is why each member of the Body must be dealt with individually. Ministry to each member must be custom-made. Developing saints is not an assembly line operation. It is a great adventure to be part of the developing of these new creations of our Creator God. But this adventure involves the problems inherent in dealing with such a variety of gifts and ministries.

This may be illustrated by the oft-repeated story of the blind men and the elephant. Five blind men met an elephant. Each examined him from his own vantage point. One got hold of the tail. He said, "This elephant is like a rope."

Another felt of the trunk and announced, "The elephant is like a large snake." A third examined one of the legs of the elephant and said, "The elephant is like a tree." The fourth blind man moved his hands over the side of the elephant and decided that he was like a wall. Finally, the fifth man got hold of the elephant's ear. He proclaimed, "The elephant is like a large fan."

Each man described the elephant accurately according to his perception. They had a choice then of either arguing with one another about these various perceptions, or of putting all of their perceptions together and discovering what the elephant was really like. This is a parable of believers and their perceptions of the ministry of the Holy Spirit. Are we going to confine the Spirit's ministry to our own perception? Or, will we minister to one another faithfully until we all come to a full-orbed view of the multifaceted grace of God flowing from the ministry of the Spirit?

Spiritual gifts are meant to open men to the manifold gifts of our generous God—Father, Son, and Spirit. The gift of the Father is the Son. The gift of the Son is the Spirit. The gifts of the Spirit are divine enablements. The gifts of the Church are the multifaceted grace of God. Each of these successive gifts encompasses all the previous gifts. The gift of the Son includes the gift of the Father. The gift of the Spirit embraces both of the previous gifts. The giving of the Church should therefore include all the previous gifts. She is a channel through which the gifts of grace are to flow unhindered.

Each believer views the church and its ministry through the eyes of his gifts. This means that every member has his own perception of the status and needs of the church. This holds great potential for conflict.

The harmonizing of the gifts requires that we take people with infinitely diverse concepts and concerns and put them together into a symphony of divine activity. For example, look at a church where a prophet and pastor are engaged together in equipping the believers. The prophet sees the need for correction, for his gift is a corrective gift. He looks at the church through the eyes of a prophet. He sees doctrinal deviations. He quickly observes signs of corporate backsliding. His prophetic gift strongly colors the perception he has of this church.

The pastor, on the other hand, sees the need for confirmation. He sees a group of people who need to be confirmed in the faith. They need to be fed and strengthened. He does not quickly observe the doctrinal deviations nor the need for correction; he has the heart and eyes of a shepherd. Both men are looking at the same congregation of believers. The prophet says, "They need correction." Looking at the same church, the pastor says, "They need nurture and pastoral care so that they can grow strong and healthy Christian lives." Unless these two persons recognize not only their own gifts and perceptions, but also the gifts and perceptions of the other person, a conflict can develop between these two equipping ministry gifts. Both of them see properly the needs of the church, but they both see through the eyes of their spiritual gifts.

Another example would be in a situation where an evangelist and a teacher are working together to minister health and growth in a church. The evangelist has his own set of questions. How many people have been saved this past year? How can we motivate the saints to get out into the community and witness? How many believers will respond to a call for house-to-house visitation and witnessing? He is primarily concerned about additions to the church.

The teacher has another set of questions: What kind of Christian education program do we have? How much do the people know about the Bible? Who is responsible for developing the training program for new converts? Why should we get them saved and then fail to teach them the Bible? Both men are concerned about the welfare of the church. But one thinks primarily about outreach and new converts, while the other is especially concerned about growth and development of the present membership.

Or observe a committee at work where one member has the gift of administration and another has the gift of exhortation. The first is occupied with plans, strategies, and careful reporting. The second is just as occupied with encouraging individuals in the congregation. One is carefully organized, while the other is much more impulsive in his activities. It is not that one is more spiritual than the other. Rather, the two attitudes are determined primarily by the spiritual gifts of the persons involved. Each one wants to do what his gift motivates him to do for the church. The evangelist wants to convert. The prophet wants to correct. The pastor wants to confirm. The exhorter wants to bless the church. The teacher wants to instruct the church. Various gift mixes pose similar kinds of perception problems.

The apostle/evangelist has one concern and that is the multiplying of believers and churches. He sees continually through the eyes of an apostle and an evangelist. How many people have been saved? How many churches have been planted? Those are his questions. This person may irritate other members of the church by continually pressing those questions. Working beside the apostle/evangelist is a pastor-exhorter, who primarily wants to mature believers. He is interested in feeding the flock and healing the members. While he may welcome the multiplication of believers and churches, that is not his first concern. He gives most of his attention to tending the sheep. He is more concerned about the churches already planted than about planting new ones. The apostle/evangelist involved in multiplying believers and planting churches may tend to overlook the ministry of the pastor/exhorter.

The pastor/exhorter, on the other hand, can become so concerned with maturing the congregation that he loses the vision of the evangelist and the church planter. It is the responsibility of those in leadership in the church to bring these various gifts into a symphony of divine ministry that will edify the church. This means blending diverse personalities into a ministry team.

The administrator is systematic and analytical in his way of thinking, while the exhorter is spontaneous and emotional in the way he serves. There is nothing wrong with either one of these persons. Both are highly motivated and deeply committed to the building of the church. But they can easily come into conflict because of their diverse viewpoints. Each may have difficulty recognizing and respecting the valid ministry of the other.

The conflict between Paul and Barnabas, as recorded in Acts 15:36-41, may well have been caused by the spiritual gifts of these two great men. Paul was an apostle, a highly disciplined church planter, who placed great emphasis upon faithfulness and dependability. Barnabas was called "the son of exhortation." He was among other things an exhorter. In fact, Paul would not have been in Antioch had it not been for this gift in Barnabas. Barnabas, looking through the eyes of a pastor/exhorter, could not follow Paul's decision. Thus, the sharp dissension between these two great friends.

How many times has this happened in the church? How many conflicts have developed because the parties involved were viewing a situation through the eyes of their own gifts and ministries, while failing to perceive the ministries and gifts of others in the church? It is important for the equipping ministries in the church to view the church in the light of its total ministry. This broad view is essential if the church is to be developed into a healthy body.

There is diversity even in the leadership. There is an apostolic ministry, a prophetic ministry, an evangelistic ministry, and a pastoral ministry. And these ministries must be blended together and function in harmony with each other. They must not conflict. While there may be apparent conflicts in the ministries of these leaders, these conflicts must be brought under the authority of the Word of God. The unity of the Spirit, who is the Author of all spiritual gifts, must eliminate all dissension that would cripple the church.

When God sends the prophet with his corrective ministry to the church, all the other ministries give a wholehearted "Amen!" to his ministry. Each equipper exercises his gift as a musician would play his instrument in a symphony orchestra. Each has his notes to sound. Each has his solo parts to play. But all the instruments and music blend into a beautiful song of worship and praise unto God.

Gifts also help to determine the participants in the various programs of the church. Not all members will relate to specific programs. The interest and involvement of the members will depend to a great extent upon their spiritual gifts.

For example, the church inaugurates a new visitation and outreach program. The pastor may insist that everybody participates. He may even impose a guilt trip on all who fail to engage in his new thrust in evangelism. But try as he may, some of the believers will never fit into this ministry. Later the church may launch a program for ministering to the elderly in the community. The participants in this program will vary from that in the previous one. This also applies to the financial supporters for various ministries. Some will give generously to support education but give little to evangelism. Others will give to benevolence but will give little to building projects. It is important to give each person an opportunity to minister in the realm of his special interest.

Every member of the church has a ministry. It is the task of the equippers, with the guidance of the Holy Spirit, to help each person find his place. This can be illustrated by two unique examples.

Tom Smith had attended church from a child, but he had never held any position in the church. Because of poor eyesight (even as a child), he could scarcely read and write his name. He would attend Sunday school but would not attend class, searching for some odd job to keep him busy during the Sunday school hour, because teachers had embarrassed him by insisting that he read in class. So he was something of a misfit.

As the church grew, Tom's pastor saw the need for a well organized team of ushers. He appointed Tom as chairman of this team. For the first time in his life, Tom had an important job in the church. He assumed his responsibilities with the zeal of a rookie on a major league baseball team. He carried out his duties with a faithfulness that amazed his pastor, who never again had to worry about ushers being ready to do their job. He served in this position with pride and efficiency. The church had discovered his gift after years of ignoring this valuable member of the Body.

Another example is Shirley Robinson. She, too, had been something of a misfit. She had never held any position in the church. She was not a teacher. She never spoke in public. She was not the type of person to send out visiting for the church.

But she was a very efficient secretary with a public utility company.

Her gifts were discovered during a special visitation campaign. When the work became too much for the staff, the pastor approached her about helping with the records and mailings. She grumbled somewhat half-heartedly but agreed to help. The pastor soon learned that the mild complaining was just a cover up. She loved every minute of the work. For the first time in her life, she became vitally involved in the work of the church. After working eight hours on her job, she would often spend five or six hours working at the church. Many times she worked till after midnight in order to get out a mailing. The growth of the church would have been greatly hindered but for Shirley's faithful labors. Some of the leaders in the church had trouble adjusting to her critical evaluations of the church's record keeping and filing system, but they soon learned that she could be a vital member of the team. While she had a great deal to learn about working with others, she was sincerely committed to serving the Lord.

These two examples should help us to understand better the importance of finding a ministry for everyone in the church, even those with complex personality traits. Nothing is more important in the equipping ministry given to the church than to understand that everybody is somebody important. Everybody should become a vital part of the church. It is a tragic loss to the church when certain people are ignored and left out of the ministry life of the Body.

The mending, healing, restoring ministry of the equipping ministry gifts is essential if all members are to play the same song, if there is to be harmony rather than discord.

STUDY QUESTIONS FOR CHAPTER 5

1. List the twenty spiritual gifts defined in this chapter and place them in their categories.

2. What are the five characteristics of ministry gifts?

3. What are the five characteristics of manifestation gifts?

4. Why is it necessary to harmonize the gifts?

CHAPTER SIX

———————◆———————

Manifestation Gifts

The manifestation gifts of the Spirit are listed in 1 Corinthians 12:8-10. The Greek word which is translated "manifestation" in verse seven is *phanerosis*. The verb *phaneroo,* according to Thayer, means "to make manifest or visible or known what has been hidden or unknown, to manifest, whether by words or deed, or in any other way . . ." (Thayer, J. H., *Greek-English Lexicon of the New Testament,* Zondervan, 1977, pp. 648, 649). Strong says, "To render apparent . . . exhibition . . . expression" (Strong, James, *Exhaustive Concordance of the Bible,* Abingdon, 1980, p 75 in "Greek Dictionary of the New Testament"). The root, *phan,* signifies shining or *outshining.*

The manifestations in this passage are supernatural expressions of the presence of the Holy Spirit in the church. These are "surprises of the Spirit" which exhibit His divine activity in the ministry of the church. Look again at 1 Corinthians 12:4-10:

> Now there are varieties of gifts, but the same Spirit. And there are varieties of ministries, and the same Lord. And there are varieties of effects, but the same God who works all things in all persons. But to each one is given the manifestation of the Spirit for the common good. For to one is given the word of wisdom through the Spirit, and to another the word of knowledge according to the same Spirit; to another faith by the same Spirit, and to another gifts of heal-

ing by the one Spirit, and to another the effecting of miracles, and to another prophecy, and to another the distinguishing of spirits, to another various kinds of tongues, and to another the interpretation of tongues. But one and the same Spirit works all these things, distributing to each one individually just as He wills (NASB).

Here we have a list of nine manifestations of the Spirit. These expressions of the Spirit's presence are divine out-shinings that give encouragement to the church and enhance the proclamation of the gospel. They cannot be programmed or preplanned, but are spontaneous manifestations of the Divine Comforter. These gifts are "the gifts of the Spirit" which were brought back into prominence in the church by the classical Pentecostal Movement during the early part of the twentieth century. They are part of the ministry of the Holy Spirit in a truly New Testament church.

CHARACTERISTICS

Let us review the characteristics of manifestation gifts.

(1) The manifestation gifts are temporary. Once the manifestation is over, the gift is no longer the possession of the individual. Individuals do not possess manifestation gifts. They are simply channels for those manifestations.

(2) These manifestation gifts have no relationship to natural abilities. A person may be used of God in an area that he would never be used in a natural sense. This is a supernatural manifestation. For example, a person who would never preach a sermon may give a prophetic utterance by the Spirit.

(3) These gifts have little relationship to one's position in the body of Christ. Any person in the Body may be used by the Spirit for the manifestation of any of these gifts. Consequently, the gift is emphasized and not the person. The manifestation must not become a badge of super spirituality.

(4) The Body is to receive and rejoice in these surprises of the Spirit.

DEFINITIONS

Let us look at these manifestation gifts of the Spirit and give a brief definition of each one.

(1) A Word of Wisdom.

Notice the indefinite article, *a*. It is unfortunate that most translations of this passage read "*the* word of wisdom." There is no definite article in the Greek text. It should read "*a* word of wisdom." The difference between *the* and *a* is very important here.

Our definition of this gift clarifies why this reads in the Greek text "a word of wisdom": A word of wisdom is a supernatural utterance of a *specific* word, given at a *specific* time, giving God's wisdom to a *specific* situation. It usually provides an answer to a vexing problem in the church—an answer that unites and edifies the church. It is a manifestation of the Spirit in which God gives a member of the church a word of wisdom far beyond his natural wisdom. The person through whom this word is given may be one who is not known for great wisdom.

An example of this occurred at the Jerusalem Council (Acts 15). A crisis arose in the early church. The conflict between the Jewish believers and the new Gentile believers threatened to divide the church. They gathered to consider this matter. After much debate and apostolic testimony, James says, "For it seemed good to the Holy Ghost, and to us, to lay upon you no greater burden than these necessary things" (v. 28). It seems evident that the Holy Spirit gave a word of wisdom to resolve this budding conflict. The solution was an ingenious compromise between the two factions that allowed the church to continue its remarkable expansion among the Gentiles. This manifestation gift then has provided supernatural wisdom for difficult circumstances in the course of church history.

(2) A Word of Knowledge.

Note again the indefinite article, *a*. It is *a* manifestation of the Holy Spirit in which God imparts to a member of the body of Christ information or facts which only God may know in order to assist the church in a special time of need.

An illustration of this is found in Acts 5: Ananias and Sapphira, evidently wanting the same kind of recognition and honor that Barnabas had received because of his gift to the church, devised a plan to deceive the infant church into believing that they, too, had given all to the church.

It seems that other than Ananias and Sapphira only God knew about this deception. But when Ananias brought the money to the church, a manifestation of the Spirit was given. A surprise of the Spirit rescued the young church from this deception.

Seemingly on the spur of the moment, Simon Peter knew something that he could never have learned apart from the manifestation of the Spirit. The Holy Spirit told him exactly what had happened, sharing with him just a bit of God's omniscience. This was a word of knowledge—a knowledge about that person that only God knew.

This is what happens when a member of the Body suddenly and inexplicably knows the physical, spiritual, or financial need of another member of the Body. This enables him to minister to that need.

While there are charlatans who practice deception along this line in order to amass gain for themselves, there is a genuine word of knowledge in which God, in His divine grace and graciousness, manifests Himself by giving facts or information that could not be known except by a supernatural manifestation of the Spirit. This does not mean that the person who is used in this way suddenly becomes a knowledgeable person. It may be someone with limited knowledge whom God uses to manifest a word of knowledge.

(3) Faith.

This is not normal Christian faith. This is not the faith by which we are saved, not saving faith. Nor is it the faith by which the believer lives. It is a special gift of faith bestowed upon a member of the Body to enable its recipient to carry out some special task of ministry. This often involves moving with confidence and steadfastness toward a humanly impossible goal. Here is a manifestation of a special type of faith to lay hold of some special project that God wants to accomplish in the world.

The Holy Spirit gives a vision of what He wants done. The person who is given this manifestation of faith receives assurance that it will come to pass.

It may be that no one but that person believes that this task can be accomplished. But he moves ahead with confidence that it is going to come to pass. This is illustrated by the faith of the apostle Paul in the journey to Rome as recorded in Acts 27. Though all of the circumstances pointed toward a great loss of lives in the storm, Paul said, "There shall be no loss of any man's life among you . . . for I believe God" (vv. 22, 25). Paul had a word from the Lord and, as a result, a special gift of faith. This was not faith for *all* ships in *all* storms, but it was for this *specific* ship in this *specific* storm.

It is amazing how a person who is used in a manifestation of the gift of faith in one circumstance can be so faithless at another time in a similar circumstance. This is a clear indication that this is not something that is given to a person as a permanent gift. It is a special faith that the Spirit in His supernatural working gives to a particular person at a particular time to meet a particular need. This manifestation is often needed to rebuild broken down churches or to restore divided churches. God by His Spirit must reveal Himself in order to accomplish what seems impossible.

(4) Gifts of Healings.

In 1 Corinthians 12:28 both of these words are plural — gifts of healings. This is one of the manifestations most desired by men. It is also a much abused gift. No other gifts have been more exploited by unscrupulous men than the gifts of healings.

Gifts of healings are manifestations of the Spirit of God by which God ministers healing to members of the body of Christ. Every healing is a fresh gift. Every manifestation is a fresh gift of healing. There is no scriptural basis for claiming a ministry of healing. It is a manifestation gift. Now that does not mean that there are not people who are used mightily in the area of healing. Nor does it mean that there are not people who, because of their prophetic or evangelistic ministry, do not have manifold healings in their ministries.

But there is no scriptural evidence for a special ministry of healing.

Every healing is a fresh manifestation and may be given through any member of the Body. These manifestations have a twofold purpose:

(1) They are given to provide healing to the body of Christ. God delights in the health of His people, and the Holy Spirit delights in ministering healing.

(2) The gifts of healings are given to confirm the preaching of the gospel (Mark 16:20). So the gifts of healings often accompany the church planting ministry of the apostles. Pioneer missionaries need these signs following the proclamation of the Word.

The gifts of healings are far more comprehensive than many think. Emphasis is given most of the time to physical healing, and the vast majority of requests for prayer for healing have to do with the diseases and infirmities of the body. But gifts of healings cover the needs of the whole man. People need healing spiritually. They need healing emotionally. Some need their memories healed of the scars and the hurts of the past. Healing then becomes the healing of the whole person — spirit, soul, and body.

Many physical maladies have their roots in psychological problems. These too need healing. The church needs to be much more comprehensive in its understanding of the manifestations of healing. We need to see that God has made provision for the healing of the total man.

Those used most frequently in the gifts of healings see only a fraction of those ministered to healed. Those who pray for thousands see only a small percentage of the people healed. This manifestation is not given to any individual to use as he wills, but it may be given to any member of the church as the Spirit wills.

Several years ago I was in a five-week revival in Salem, Virginia, during which there were many manifestations of the Spirit. We frequently had prayer for the sick, and many people were mightily and miraculously healed.

One night after praying for those who came forward, I had the distinct feeling in my spirit that there were others in the congregation who needed healing. I said, "God is able to heal you right where you are. And if you want someone to minister to you, turn to a Christian near you and ask him to lay hands on you for healing."

A dear member of that congregation turned to another member of the church and said, "I should have gone forward for prayer, but I didn't. Would you lay hands on me?" The lady to whom she turned had never prayed for the sick nor had she ever laid hands on anyone to minister healing. But that night in that crowded church building she laid her hands on her sister in the Lord, and God instantly healed her.

(5) Miracles.

This is the manifestation of supernatural power given to the servant of God to authenticate the preaching of the Word. According to Mark 16:17 believers do not follow miracles; miracles follow believers. The miraculous follows the believing of the Word.

The man who supposedly performs miracles to show people what a great man of God he is contradicts the very Scriptures he may use to support his claims. Miracles done through the power of the Spirit will have as their primary purpose the confirmation of the Word of God being proclaimed. They are never intended to be instruments for the advancement or exaltation of the human instrument being used.

(6) Prophecy.

Prophecy is the manifestation of a spontaneously uttered word from the Lord given through any member of the Body for the encouragement, edification, or exhortation of the church. This is the one gift that is both a ministry and a manifestation. We have already discussed the ministry gift of prophet. However, there is a manifestation gift of prophecy which is not necessarily given through the prophet.

This type of manifestation is not confined to the New Testament. When Samuel anointed Saul to be King over Israel, Saul prophesied (1 Samuel 10:1-12). "Is Saul also among the prophets?" became a proverb in Israel. Saul was never a prophet. It was the coming of the Spirit of God upon him that caused him to utter a prophetic word.

Often the person used to give a prophetic word will be someone totally foreign to the prophetic ministry in the church. But God will give him a prophetic utterance. This is the manifestation gift of prophecy. It is different from the equipping ministry gift of prophet.

(7) Discerning of Spirits.

This is the manifestation of the Spirit which enables a member of the Body to determine with supernatural confidence the spiritual source of the conduct or message of a prophet or teacher. This gift is widely misunderstood in the church. Some confuse it with the manifestation of a *word of knowledge*. Any manifestation that reveals the need of a person is a word of knowledge, not the discerning of spirits. The discerning of spirits is the ability to discern the spiritual source of a message or of a teaching.

There are three spiritual sources: the divine Spirit, demonic spirits, and human spirits. The discerning of spirits is that supernatural ability given by the Holy Spirit in a specific situation to enable a person to determine which of these three is the source of a prophetic utterance. Any time there is a manifestation of prophecy, tongues, or interpretation of tongues that has its source in either demonic or human spirits, someone should receive the gift of the discerning of spirits.

The final two manifestation gifts are the only two which are new to the church age. All others may be found in the Bible prior to the Day of Pentecost.

(8) Tongues.

This is the manifestation of the Spirit which enables a person to speak to the church in a language he does not understand and which is incomprehensible to the hearers. This manifestation is not found anywhere in the Old or New Testament prior to the Day of Pentecost. In this manifestation a person speaks a language which he does not understand and which he has never studied. This is distinctly a pentecostal gift. It is new to this age and has been a source of much controversy in the church. It is, however, the distinctive badge of pentecostal believers.

(9) Interpretation of Tongues.

The gift of interpretation of tongues is the companion of the gift of tongues. It is the manifestation of the Spirit which must accompany the manifestation of tongues, giving the meaning of what has been spoken in tongues.

We have a responsibility with regard to these manifestations. We are to be sensitive to the Holy Spirit. Paul wrote to the church at Thessalonica, "Despise not prophesyings. Prove all things; hold fast that which is good" (1 Thessalonians 5:20, 21). He was talking about these manifestation gifts. The *New International Version (NIV)* reads, ". . . do not treat prophecies with contempt." Don't reject prophecies just because you have heard some counterfeit prophecies, but test them by the Word of God. Not only are we to test them, but we are to hold fast to that which is good and genuine.

A church cannot be a full-orbed New Testament church without being open and sensitive to the manifestations of the Spirit. We need to be willing to receive and rejoice in these manifestation gifts of the Spirit. These surprises of the Spirit can encourage and edify believers when they are allowed to operate within the guidelines given to us in Holy Scripture.

STUDY QUESTIONS FOR CHAPTER 6

1. Give biblical examples of the manifestations of a word of wisdom and a word of knowledge.

2. Define the manifestation of discerning of spirits.

3. What manifestations are unique to the pentecostal age?

4. List the nine manifestation gifts.

CHAPTER SEVEN

—————◆—————

The Initial Evidence of the Fullness of the Spirit

The nine manifestation gifts of the Spirit may be divided into three groups. Three of them have to do with perception, three with performance, and three with proclamation—seeing, doing, and speaking.

A word of knowledge, a word of wisdom, and the discerning of spirits have to do with perception. Faith, healings, and miracles have to do with performance. Tongues, interpretation, and prophecy have to do with proclamation.

All of these nine manifestations of the Spirit, except tongues and interpretation of tongues, are found in the Scripture prior to Pentecost . These twin gifts are distinctly associated with the pentecostal age. They are unique gifts for the church age. They are also the subject of controversy in the church. Much of the controversy stems from a lack of knowledge on the part of much of the church. No wonder Paul wrote, "Now concerning spiritual gifts, brethren, I would not have you ignorant" (1 Corinthians 12:1).

It is important to distinguish between tongues as the initial evidence of the fullness of the Spirit and tongues as a manifestation gift of the Spirit. Classical pentecostals have held consistently to the position that speaking with tongues is the initial evidence of the fullness of the Spirit. There are those who reject this position, holding to the view that tongues are given to only a few Spirit-filled believers.

FIVE BIBLICAL ACCOUNTS

What does the Bible have to say about this question? The Scripture is our final authority. Five instances are recorded in the book of Acts where people are filled with the Spirit. (1) Pentecost.

The first example is found in Acts 2:1-4:

> And when the day of Pentecost had come, they were all together in one place. And suddenly there came from heaven a noise like a violent, rushing wind, and it filled the whole house where they were sitting. And there appeared to them tongues as of fire distributing themselves, and they rested on each one of them. And they were all filled with the Holy Spirit and began to speak with other tongues, as the Spirit was giving them utterance (NASB).

This is the record of the initial outpouring of the Holy Spirit. The promise of the Father was poured out upon 120 waiting believers. They were all filled with the Holy Spirit and began to speak with tongues as the Spirit gave the utterance. It is clear that *all* who were filled spoke with tongues. If it were true that only some who are filled with the Spirit speak with tongues, why would all of those filled in that initial outpouring speak with tongues? Was this the pattern for the New Testament age?

(2) Samaria.

The second account of the Holy Spirit baptism recorded in the book of Acts is the story of the Samaritan pentecost:

> Now when the apostles in Jerusalem heard that Samaria had received the word of God, they sent them Peter and John, who came down and prayed for them, that they might receive the Holy Spirit. For He had not yet fallen upon any of them; they had simply been baptized in the name of the Lord Jesus. Then they began laying their hands on them, and they were receiving the Holy Spirit. Now when Simon saw that the Spirit was bestowed through the laying on of the

apostles' hands, he offered them money, saying, "Give this authority to me as well, so that everyone on whom I lay my hands may receive the Holy Spirit" (8:14-19, NASB).

This passage does not say specifically that the Samaritans spoke with tongues, but even non-pentecostal scholars have agreed that the language used in verse 18 indicates that they did speak with tongues. It was when "Simon saw that the Spirit was bestowed" that he sought to purchase this power. What did Simon see? The verb translated "saw" is the Greek word *idon* which means to perceive, notice, discern, or discover by any of the senses. Simon already had seen miracles of healings and exorcisms. What did he experience here that was different?

F. F. Bruce, one of the great New Testament scholars of our day, has this comment: "The context leaves us in no doubt that the reception of the Spirit was attended by external manifestations such as had marked His descent on the earliest disciples at Pentecost" (*The Book of Acts, New International Commentary,* p. 181).

The renowned Baptist scholar, Dr. A. T. Robertson, wrote: "This participle which is the second aorist active of *horao* shows plainly that those who received the gift of the Holy Spirit spoke with tongues" (*Word Pictures in the New Testament, III*, p. 107). This great New Testament scholar was certainly not a defender of pentecostal doctrine, but he agrees that in this particular instance these Samaritans spoke with tongues. The evidence indicates that the Samaritans spoke with tongues just as the 120 did on the Day of Pentecost.

(3) Paul.

In Acts 9:17-19 we read the account of Paul's pentecost:
And Ananias departed and entered the house, and after laying his hands on him said, "Brother Saul, the Lord Jesus, who appeared to you on the road by which you were coming, has sent me so that you may regain your sight, and be filled with the Holy Spirit." And immediately there fell from his eyes something like scales, and he regained his sight, and he arose and

was baptized; and he took food and was strengthened (NASB).

We find no reference here to Paul's speaking with tongues. In fact, if this were all the evidence we had, this passage could pose a problem. There is not a single verse in this 9th chapter that says Paul spoke with tongues when he was filled with the Spirit. But we have other evidence. In 1 Corinthians 14:5 Paul writes to the charismatic Corinthians, "Now I wish that you all spoke in tongues" (NASB). It is difficult to believe that Paul would wish for something contrary to the New Testament pattern. He desired that they all speak with tongues. He goes on in verse 18 to testify, "I thank God, that I speak with tongues more than you all" (NASB). This is his clear-cut testimony. There is no question about it, Paul spoke with tongues. Verse 15 tells us that he was accustomed to singing and praying in tongues.

(4) Caesarea.

The fourth account in the book of Acts of believers being filled with the Spirit is found in Acts 10:44-46:

> While Peter was still speaking these words, the Holy Spirit fell upon all those who were listening to the message. And all the circumcised believers who had come with Peter were amazed, because the gift of the Holy Spirit had been poured out upon the Gentiles also. For they were hearing them speaking with tongues and exalting God (NASB).

How were they sure that these people had been filled with the Spirit? Because they heard them speaking with tongues.

This scriptural account of the Caesarean pentecost states plainly that the convincing evidence that the people in the house of Cornelius had been filled with the Spirit was the fact that they spoke with tongues. This is so clear that it is difficult to imagine anyone attempting to deny it.

(5) Ephesus.

The account of the Ephesian pentecost is recorded in Acts 19:1-6:

> And it came about that while Apollos was at Corinth, Paul having passed through the upper country came to Ephesus, and found some disciples, and

he said to them, "Did you receive the Holy Spirit when you believed?" And they said to him, "No we have not even heard whether there is a Holy Spirit." And he said, "Into what then were ye baptized?" And they said, "Into John's baptism." And Paul said, "John baptized with the baptism of repentance, telling the people to believe in Him who was coming after him, that is, in Jesus." And when they heard this, they were baptized in the name of the Lord Jesus. And when Paul had laid his hands upon them, the Holy Spirit came on them, and they began speaking with tongues and prophesying (NASB).

Here again, in the fifth example in the book of Acts of people being filled with the Spirit, we are told clearly that they spoke with tongues. And the reason that the apostle Paul could say that they were filled with the Spirit was that they spoke with tongues.

Now as we look at these five examples, we see that three of the accounts clearly and specifically state that they spoke with tongues. In fact, it is evident in two cases that the proof given that they were filled with the Spirit was that they spoke with tongues. In the two instances where tongues is not specifically mentioned, there is overwhelming evidence that they too spoke with tongues.

The proof is compelling that in each of the five instances in the book of Acts, the initial evidence for the fullness of the Spirit was speaking with tongues as the Spirit gave utterance.

THREE ADDITIONAL REASONS

(1) Paul's Teaching.

Paul's words to the believers at Corinth are also a strong indication that tongues were meant for all believers. He said in 1 Corinthians 14:5, "I would that ye all spake with tongues." Would it not be strange for Paul to say to these Corinthians, "I wish that you all spoke in tongues," if tongues were not meant as a universal gift to believers? This is not referring to the manifestation gift, but to tongues as a means of worship for the individual.

In verse 23 he implies that they all do speak with tongues when he writes, "If therefore the whole church should assemble together and all speak in tongues…" (NASB). This indicates that all of them were tongues-speakers. The whole context of 1 Corinthians 14 is based upon this premise. That seems to be evidence of the universal manifestation of tongues in those that are filled with the Spirit. Paul's counsel in this chapter is to give them guidelines for the exercise of this gift.

(2) Tongues Unique to the Pentecostal Age.

The uniqueness of tongues is also revealed by the fact that all other manifestations of the Spirit can be found either in the Old Testament or the New Testament prior to Pentecost. Tongues, with its companion gift of interpretation, is the one new manifestation. Furthermore, it was the first, or initial, manifestation. The others followed.

This is another reason for believing that tongues is the initial evidence of the fullness of the Spirit. This unique gift, a distinctive of the pentecostal age, is still the first confirmation of the fullness of the Spirit.

All believers have the Holy Spirit. The Bible makes clear that one cannot be a Christian without having the Spirit (Romans 8:9). It is the Spirit who convicts us of sin. It is the Spirit who converts us to Christ. It is the Spirit who sanctifies us. It is the Spirit who administers all of the grace of God in the lives of believers.

Jesus told His disciples in John 14:17, " . . . ye know him; for he dwelleth with you, and shall be in you." The Holy Spirit was no stranger to the disciples. They knew Him. He had indeed been at work in their lives. But they were soon to experience a new dimension of His work which would be accompanied by the manifestation of tongues.

(3) The Tongue Is the Most Unruly Member.

Another reason for believing in tongues as the initial evidence of the fullness of the Spirit is that it is a symbol of the Spirit's complete control of the believer. Tongues gives evidence that the whole person is yielded to God. The most unruly member of the human body is the tongue. James says,

"But the tongue can no man tame; it is an unruly evil, full of deadly poison" (James 3:8).

Someone has said that the last two things that are converted are the tongue and the pocketbook. If the fullness of the Spirit means the coming of the Spirit to take possession of the believer so that he becomes the instrument of the Spirit, then what better evidence could there be than that the Spirit uses the human tongue to express praise to God in a language totally unknown to the speaker? The human tongue thus becomes the supernatural instrument of praise.

These reasons clearly indicate that speaking with other tongues as the Spirit gives utterance is the initial evidence of the fullness of the Spirit.

DIVINE-HUMAN ACTIVITY

Speaking with tongues is a divine-human activity. Man cannot do it without the Holy Spirit and the Holy Spirit does not do it without man's cooperation. The Holy Spirit gives the utterance, but the human agent must do the speaking. Many people labor under the false impression that the Holy Spirit does the speaking and that man has no control over the vocal expression. In each instance in the New Testament the account states that the human recipients of the fullness of the Spirit did the speaking. Acts 2:4 says that they spake as the Spirit gave the utterance. The utterance must come from the Holy Spirit, but the speaking must be done by the individual. (1) Not All Human.

There are two unscriptural positions taken concerning the matter. Both are extreme emphases upon only one element of tongues speaking. First, some people claim the ability to teach others to speak with tongues. They give the words to the person and ask him to repeat them. That certainly is not in harmony with the Scriptures. One cannot teach another person to speak with tongues. This effort to manipulate the Holy Spirit and believers is both dangerous and deceiving. (2) Not All Divine.

On the other hand, there are those who go to the other extreme and are just as unscriptural. They teach that one does not speak himself; the Holy Spirit does the speaking. Many sincere seekers after the fullness of the Spirit have waited fruitlessly for years to experience such an expression of tongues. It never comes, and they eventually despair of ever being filled with the Spirit. God does not operate like that. God does not make robots out of people. He works through His children as they yield to Him. He does not violate man's will. The devil will use people against their will, but God will not. When the Holy Spirit comes into an individual, He does so because that person receives Him. He will not force Himself in. The Holy Spirit is a gentleman. He will only go where He is wanted. That is why we are urged not to grieve the Spirit (Ephesians 4:30).

The Holy Spirit does not overrule the will of man. If one wills to be saved, he can be saved. No person is ever saved against his will. Neither will one be filled with the Spirit against his will. He must willingly submit to the Holy Spirit. Furthermore, he must willingly give expression to tongues when the Spirit gives utterance. The language is from the Spirit—He gives the utterance—but there must be a point where in faith the individual gives expression to that utterance.

For one person to manipulate another person into speaking in tongues is deceptive. But at the same time, to lead a person to believe that he has no part in responding to the Spirit and giving expression to the utterance that the Holy Spirit gives to him would also be deceptive. It can lead that sincere believer into a lifetime of frustrated "tarrying" for the Spirit because he is expecting the Holy Spirit to do what He will never do.

Speaking with tongues requires both the supernatural utterance of the Spirit and the intelligent response of the believer. In yielding to the Spirit one may surrender himself completely to the promptings of the Spirit. He may be keenly aware of the supernatural power that gives him the language. But he should always be conscious of his willing response to these promptings. If he loses control and feels helpless to either respond or refuse to respond,

80

it would be wise for him to try the spirit which is using him. The Holy Spirit does not force people to do anything contrary to their will.

STUDY QUESTIONS FOR CHAPTER 7

1. How may the nine manifestation gifts be divided into three groups of three?

2. How many accounts are there in the book of Acts of people being filled with the Spirit? How many of these accounts say that they spoke with tongues?

3. How do we know that Paul spoke with tongues?

4. Why is tongues such a good sign of being filled with the Spirit?

CHAPTER EIGHT

Three Kinds of Tongues

S peaking with tongues has been the subject of great interest, as well as great controversy, in the church for the past three-quarters of a century.

One of the chief causes of controversy is the failure to distinguish between the different kinds of tongues which are manifested through the Spirit-filled believer. Many people do not realize that there is a difference between tongues as the *initial evidence of being filled with the Spirit, devotional tongues,* and the *manifestation of tongues* in a congregation of believers. When the distinction is not made between these three kinds of tongues, much confusion can result.

INITIAL EVIDENCE

The previous chapter dealt with tongues as the *initial evidence* of the infilling of the Spirit. The evidence indicates that a person who is filled with the Spirit will speak with tongues. This is the sign both to him and to the church that he has been filled with the Spirit.

The book of Acts indicates that all those who were filled with the Spirit in the New Testament spoke with tongues. This is the initial evidence, though not the only evidence. In fact, there may be other evidences more important in the long run. But in His providence, God has chosen tongues as the initial evidence that the Spirit has taken possession of the believer.

DEVOTIONAL TONGUES

Now we want to look at a second kind of tongues which we will call *devotional tongues*. Devotional tongues are given to the believer to aid him in his worship of God. Examples of this are found throughout the New Testament. There are scriptural bases for praying in tongues, praising in tongues, singing in tongues, and interceding in tongues.

(1) Praying in Tongues.

In Ephesians 6:18 we read: "With all prayer and petition pray at all times in the Spirit . . . ." The same kind of phrase is used in Jude 20 where we are told to build ourselves up by "praying in the Holy Spirit . . . ." Many people believe that "praying in the Spirit" means praying in tongues. This certainly harmonizes with Paul's statement in 1 Corinthians 14:15 where he says, "I will pray with the spirit, and I will pray with the understanding . . . ."

I know of no other way to interpret Paul's language except that he prayed in tongues. How else would he contrast praying with the Spirit and praying with the understanding? The context also gives strong evidence that he is dealing here with speaking in tongues.

Praying in tongues is praying with the spirit. Our understanding is bypassed, and we express the mind of God in languages we do not know. One's prayers are generally limited to his vocabulary and understanding, but praying in the spirit goes beyond these limitations. It is prayer that is not filtered and diluted by his experiences and perceptions. The Holy Spirit gives to the believer the facility to pray in languages he has never learned. This releases prayer that is unfettered by human prejudice and preconception.

Praying in the Holy Spirit brings us into a perfect harmony with heaven. Our two Comforters pray in harmony. The word *comforter, parakletos* in the Greek, is used in the Gospel of John three times to refer to the Holy Spirit. The same word is used in 1 John 2:1, speaking of the Lord Jesus Christ. It says, "we have an advocate with the Father, Jesus Christ the righteous." A comforter is a lawyer, a pleader, a helper, an intercessor.

The Holy Spirit is the Comforter here on earth indwelling the believer. Jesus is the Comforter at the right hand of the Father in heaven. Surely the interceding that Jesus does for us at the right hand of the Father will harmonize with the interceding that the Spirit does within us here on earth.

Praying in the Spirit is the believer praying according to the mind of the Holy Spirit so that his praying comes into perfect harmony with what Jesus is praying at the right hand of the Father. These two (the Son and the Spirit) unite in prayer—one on earth and the other in heaven—to bring to pass God's beautiful will for His people and His church.

(2) Praising in Tongues.

Devotional tongues may take the form of praise. The tongues on the Day of Pentecost proclaimed "the wonderful works of God" (Acts 2:11). At Caesarea, Peter and his Jewish companions heard the believers "speak with tongues, and magnify God" (Acts 10:46). Paul writes in 1 Corinthians 14:14,15:

> For if I pray in an unknown tongue, my spirit prayeth, but my understanding is unfruitful. What is it then? I will pray with the spirit, and I will pray with the understanding also: I will sing with the spirit, and I will sing with the understanding also.

What a beautiful thing it is to see a congregation of Spirit-filled believers praising the Lord! But often that praise reaches a point beyond the highest language of men. At that point the Holy Spirit transcends human language and gives an utterance in tongues that gives honor and praise and glory to God. This is a rich devotional experience for the individual and the entire congregation of believers.

(3) Singing in Tongues.

But in the same passage, he suggests a third kind of devotional tongues—singing in the Spirit. He says, "I will sing with the Spirit, and I will sing with the understanding also." In Ephesians 5:19 Paul exhorts the Spirit-filled believer to sing "psalms, and hymns, and spiritual songs." The psalms refer to Hebrew hymns recorded in the book of Psalms. The hymns were evidently songs composed by the first century saints. "Spiritual songs" were undoubtedly songs in tongues.

These are songs of praise and worship given to the believer by the Holy Spirit. The language of these songs may not be understood, but the spirit and power of such singing can be unforgettable.

(4) Intercession in Tongues.

Finally, there is *intercession in the Spirit,* found in Romans 8:26, 27: "Likewise the Spirit also helpeth our infirmities: for we know not what we should pray for as we ought: but the Spirit itself maketh intercession for us with groanings which cannot be uttered. And he that searcheth the hearts knoweth what is the mind of the Spirit, because he maketh intercession for the saints according to the will of God."

The *New International Version* reads "In the same way, the Spirit helps us in our weakness. We do not know what we ought to pray, but the Spirit himself intercedes for us with groans that words cannot express. And he who searches our hearts knows the mind of the Spirit, because the Spirit intercedes for the saints in accordance with God's will."

This intercession of the Spirit transcends human speech. The Holy Spirit pleads in prayer for the things that God wills to do. When one intercedes in tongues, he is surely engaged in supernatural intercession.

MANIFESTATION TONGUES

In 1 Corinthians 14 Paul is making a clear distinction between devotional tongues and the manifestation gift of tongues. He leaves no doubt about his speaking with tongues. He declares, "I speak with tongues more than you all." But he indicates that his tongues speaking was primarily in his devotional life. He does not eliminate the manifestation gift as part of his tongues speaking, but he does emphasize his devotional exercise of tongues—praying and singing in the Spirit.

The major part of 1 Corinthians 14, however, deals with some corrective teaching on the manifestation gift of tongues. The Corinthian church had become embroiled in controversy over the manifestation of tongues. It seems that some wanted to be free to speak in tongues anytime they felt like it. Others evidently were forbidding speaking with tongues (1 Corinthians 14:39). This matter was dividing the churches. Paul proceeded to deal with the problem. This biblical treatise on the manifestation of tongues is God's measuring rod for all pentecostals. The truths written here did not correspond with the practices of many Corinthians, but they are divine principles for all time. Man is often tempted to measure God's Word by his experience, but this is getting the cart before the horse. We must ever measure our experiences by the Word of God.

(1) Edifying the Church.

Paul begins by declaring that the object of manifestations of the Spirit is the edifying of the church. The body of Christ should always be edified when tongues are manifested in the congregation of believers. One cannot judge the appropriateness of his manifestation by whether or not he is edified individually. He must judge by whether or not the whole church is edified.

(2) Interpretation Required.

Paul asserts that there must be an interpretation. Without an interpreter the manifestation gift of tongues is lost. The body of believers must know what is being said in tongues. He states emphatically, "But if there be no interpreter, let him keep silence in the church; and let him speak to himself, and to God" (1 Corinthians 14:28).

(3) Keep Silent.

Paul places the burden for interpretation squarely on the shoulders of the one speaking in tongues. If there is no interpreter, he is to keep silent. He may speak to himself and to God—this would mean speaking quietly in tongues so as not to disturb the gathered people of God. Or, he should pray for the interpretation himself. It may be preferable to have different speakers give the tongues and the interpretation, but it surely is not out of order for the same person to give both manifestations.

Some argue that they cannot keep silent when an utterance in tongues is given to them, but Paul makes it clear that this is not true. While the Spirit gives the utterance, the believer does the speaking. He is to judge whether he is to speak aloud to the church or silently to himself and to God. Certainly Paul would have been out of order making the statements that he does in 1 Corinthians 14 if that were not true.

The Holy Spirit does not make robots out of God's people. When He indwells a person, that person does not become a mindless instrument in the hands of the Spirit. There is a reciprocal operation of the Spirit and the individual. One who says, "I cannot keep quiet! I have no control! I cannot help myself!" needs to examine his actions to determine what kind of spirit is using him. God only has volunteers. He never violates man's will.

And so, Paul first says that the manifestation of tongues must have an interpretation. But then he says that if there is no interpreter, the speaker is to keep silent. There is, of course, the added counsel, "let him speak to himself, and to God." This reveals the possibility of one's speaking in tongues quietly, in such a way that it does not disrupt a congregational meeting.

There are those who feel that any utterance given by the Spirit must be given in a loud voice. According to Paul's exhortation, this is not true. One may speak quietly to himself and to God. If the words are meant only for our Father, we can whisper quietly to Him. It is crude to speak intimate words of love and affection in a loud and boisterous tone. The love words may be for God alone—and He is not deaf.

It would be like a person in a congregation who had something to say to the person sitting next to him. He would not shout out and disrupt the service. That would be out of order. If you had a word to say to someone next to you, an urgent word that you had to speak, you would turn and whisper so that no one could hear except the person to whom you were talking.

It is important, then, for the person who has an utterance in tongues to determine whether the utterance is a manifestation to the church or a private devotional expression of tongues. Then he can judge what kind of expression to give to this utterance. Furthermore, the climate of the service will determine his response. If it is a time of corporate praise and worship, he may be able to pray or praise in tongues without disrupting the church. In fact, it may add to the climate of celebration. But if someone is preaching or teaching, he must take into account the welfare of the whole church. Will it edify the church? If not, let him keep silent.

(4) Limitation on the Number of Manifestations.

Another limitation that Paul places on the manifestation gift of tongues has to do with the number of such manifestations in any one service. Verse 27 reads: "If any man speak in an unknown tongue, let it be by two, or at the most by three, and that by course; and let one interpret." There are two interpretations of this passage. Some hold that there should be no more than two or three who speak in tongues before there is an interpretation. But the more commonly accepted view is that there should be no more than two or three manifestations of tongues in any service. If a person speaks with tongues, the church should wait for an interpretation. If no one else gives the interpretation, then the person speaking in tongues has an obligation to give the meaning of what he has said.

Paul indicates that there may be two or three messages in tongues and interpretations, but never more than that. It seems that the Corinthians had gone far beyond this limitation. They needed to set some boundaries on the exercise of this gift. It is both wise and safe, it seems to me, to limit manifestations of tongues and interpretations to no more than three in any one service. In fact, it is probably true that seldom should there be as many as three. Without infringing on the sovereignty of the Spirit, we must maintain these scriptural guidelines.

Tongues and interpretation can become a kind of toy as it had with these charismatic Corinthians. They became engrossed with tongues until that usurped the preaching of the Word. Paul issued these guidelines in order to correct an excessive emphasis on "the surprises of the Spirit"—especially tongues and interpretation.

(5) Manifestations To Be Judged.

Also these manifestations are to be judged and evaluated. No manifestation of the Spirit is to be considered infallible.

It is the duty of the congregation, and particularly the leadership of the congregation, to judge whether a word is from the Lord. Both prophecies and tongues (with interpretation) are to be judged to make sure that the word from the Lord has not been diluted or distorted by the messenger. There is nothing out of order for a pastor to step in and correct an utterance that may not be what he feels is the clear word from the Lord.

Paul makes it clear that we have this "treasure in earthen vessels" (2 Corinthians 4:7). Sometimes these clay pots garble the message God is trying to communicate. Manifestation gifts do not give infallibility to the human instruments. Therefore, we are to judge. It is not only the privilege, it is the obligation of the church to weigh and evaluate all manifestations.

We are going to come later to guidelines for evaluating and judging the manifestations of the Spirit.

(6) Forbid Not to Speak with Tongues.

Let us conclude this chapter by looking at verse 39b: " . . . forbid not to speak with tongues." The implication is that there were members in the church in Corinth who were trying to stop all speaking in tongues. Paul's word to these people is, "Stop forbidding speaking in tongues." This statement makes it perfectly clear that Paul was not trying to eliminate speaking in tongues from the Corinthian church. The answer to abuses of this gift is not the elimination of the gift. We are strictly forbidden to go this route.

Rather, we must strike a biblical balance between abuse and abolition. We must be sensitive and open to the manifestations of the Spirit. It is a sad situation when a church never has any manifestations because the people are afraid that abuses will arise. When leaders in the church are so frightened of spiritual manifestations that they stifle, if not stop, them, the church suffers tremendous loss. The leadership must teach the people to be sensitive and responsive to the manifestations of the Spirit.

But then we turn to the other side of the coin. Manifestations must be judged and evaluated. There must also be guidelines and limitations. The meetings of the church must not become one manifestation after another. This too would be unhealthy for the church.

We are to be sensitive to the Spirit. We are not to despise prophesyings, or prophetic utterances. We are not to reject the manifestations of the Spirit. We are not to forbid people to speak with tongues. But, at the same time, we are to give instructions as to when and how and in what order they are to be given. We are to judge and evaluate so that the church will be neither without manifestations nor disrupted with manifestations. What a beautiful balance can be found in the teaching of 1 Corinthians 14!

May the Lord help us to accept this teaching and to put it into practice in our assemblies. If we have not been following these clear admonitions of the apostle, may God help us to begin doing so now.

STUDY QUESTIONS FOR CHAPTER 8

1. What are the three kinds of tongues?

2. What four forms may devotional tongues take?

3. What limitations should be placed on the manifestation of tongues?

4. What warning is given in 1 Corinthians 14:39?

CHAPTER NINE

———————◆———————

Guidelines for Spiritual Manifestations

T he church has definite responsibilities with regard to the stewardship of spiritual gifts. Ministry gifts are to be discovered and developed by the church. Manifestation gifts are to be judged. One of the reasons why manifestations of tongues and prophecy, especially, have been practically eliminated from many churches is that there were no guidelines for judging and regulating such manifestations.

1 Corinthians 14 provides some basic guidelines for weighing and evaluating manifestations. A careful study of this chapter will provide a church with the proper framework within which these surprises of the Spirit must operate. Church leadership must apply these guidelines to prevent disruption and division.

Let us read 1 Corinthians 14:26-32:

> What is the outcome then, brethren? When you assemble, each one has a psalm, has a teaching, has a revelation, has a tongue, has an interpretation. Let all things be done for edification. If anyone speaks in a tongue, it should be by two or at the most three, and each in turn, and let one interpret; but if there is no interpreter, let him keep silent in the church; and let him speak to himself and to God. And let two or three prophets speak, and let the others pass judgment. But if a revelation is made to another who is seated, let

the first keep silent. For you can all prophesy one by one, so that all may learn and all may be exhorted; and the spirits of the prophets are subject to prophets for God is not a God of confusion but of peace, as in all the churches of the saints (NASB).

If this passage says anything to us, it says that it is necessary to evaluate and judge the manifestations that are given in the church. If there are tongues and interpretation, or if there is a prophetic utterance, the church must weigh these manifestations. Therefore we need some guidelines for evaluating the manifestation gifts of the Spirit.

Let us look at five guidelines by which we can judge and evaluate manifestation gifts. We can identify these five with words beginning with the letter "c." This will help us remember them.

CHRIST

If there is anything that serves as a touchstone for every ministry and every manifestation, it is the person and the work of the Lord Jesus Christ. The Holy Spirit's ministry is to reveal Christ to the believer and to develop the believer into the image of Christ. It is the mission of the Spirit to testify of Jesus Christ and to magnify Him (John 14:26; 15:26, 27; 16:13-15).

Jesus Christ is the chief cornerstone of the church. He is the chief cornerstone of spiritual gifts. Our past, our present, and our future have at the center the Lord Jesus Christ. When we look at the past, His death and His resurrection are the focal points of history for the Christian. So the Holy Spirit's ministry focuses on the death and the resurrection of Jesus Christ.

The present is filled with the exaltation of Jesus to the right hand of the Father where He ever lives to make intercession for the saints . He is the Great High Priest who intercedes for His people. And certainly at the heart of the manifestations of the Spirit is this high priestly ministry of the Lord Jesus Christ.

The future is focused on the second coming of the Lord Jesus. If we can remember that all of the manifestations of the Spirit have as their ultimate goal the person and work of the Lord Jesus Christ, that will serve as a valuable guideline to keep us from deviating from the divine pattern for spiritual gifts.

CANON

The 66 books of the Bible are referred to as "the canon of Scripture." The word *canon* is a Greek word which means "rod," or "measuring rod," a standard of measurement. Originally it referred to the standard used to judge whether or not a book was to be accepted as a part of divine revelation. It later came to mean those books which passed the test and were included in the Bible.

If we could conclude and agree that the Bible is the only infallible word from the Lord, that would serve as a tremendously important guideline for the manifestations of the Spirit. Spiritual gifts are treasured by the church, but as Paul warned the Corinthians, "we have this treasure in earthen vessels" (2 Corinthians 4:7). The picture is of some precious possession which has been housed in a clay pot. In spiritual gifts we possess divine and powerful treasures, but we possess them in clay pots. A clear understanding of this truth will help us not to give undue credence to supernatural manifestations. That is not to belittle nor disparage the manifestations of the Spirit. It is simply to put them in proper perspective.

I was shocked some time ago when talking with a pastor of a church where the manifestations of the Spirit are greatly emphasized. He kept referring to revelations in a way that made me suspect that he was giving the same value to prophecies and tongues in his church as he gave to Holy Scripture. He went on to indicate that the Scripture was not yet completed, but that God was still giving revelation just as He did to the apostles and prophets who penned Holy Scripture. That is a dangerous position. It is totally unscriptural. The canon of Scripture has been completed.

God has given to us a complete revelation in Holy Scripture. This does not mean that He will not speak to us in divine manifestations, but it does mean that all these "surprises of the Spirit" will harmonize with this infallible revelation in Holy Scripture.

We must commit ourselves completely to the authority of Scripture. The final authority is the Word of God. Many heresies have arisen in the church when infallibility has been ascribed to prophecies and revelations which should have been weighed in the balance of Holy Scripture before being accepted. Once this guideline is abandoned, the newest revelation is usually accepted as God's last word on any given subject. This means that any conflict between such revelations and Scripture will be decided in favor of the "new" revelation. So, "the measuring rod" must be used always to test the validity of spiritual manifestations.

Paul recognizes this guideline in 2 Thessalonians 2:1, 2: "And now, what about the coming again of our Lord Jesus Christ, and our being gathered together to meet him? Please don't be upset and excited, dear brothers, by the rumor that this day of the Lord has already begun. If you hear of people having visions and special messages from God about this, or letters that are supposed to have come from me, don't believe them" *(Living Bible)*

CELEBRATION

We use the word *celebration* to describe the activity of worship and praise. One of the chief duties of man is to praise God. God inhabits the praises of His people (Psalm 22:3). The psalmist exhorts everything that breathes to praise God (Psalm 150:6). It is natural then that praise and celebration should characterize pentecostal worship.

One of the things that has attracted people to the Pentecostal Movement is the quality of celebration. *The World Christian Encyclopedia,* edited by David Barrett, reveals that pentecostals are now the largest Protestant Christian group in the world. This fantastic growth has been due to a large extent to the quality of pentecostal worship.

The manifestations of the Spirit prompt and cultivate praise and worship. All over the world this is characteristic of churches where the Holy Spirit is moving. No matter what the cultural bent of a people may be, a renewal of the ministry and manifestations of the Spirit will prompt pentecostal celebration.

This is evident in the book of Acts. On the Day of Pentecost the 120 were praising and blessing God. The believers at Caesarea convinced Peter and his Jewish companions that they had been filled with the Holy Spirit because they were speaking with tongues and magnifying God—they were celebrating in typical pentecostal fashion. The manifestations of the Spirit are prompted by praise and, in turn, produce praise.

COMMUNION

The Greek word for communion is *koinonia*. That word is translated in the *King James Version* by several different English words: "fellowship," "partnership," "communion," "sharing," and "all things common." *Koinonia* is one of those words that is so full of meaning that it is hard to find any one English word to express it.

Basically, it means the "shared life of the Spirit." Two passages in the book of Acts give us an indication of what this word means. First in Acts 2:44 we read that the believers "were together, and had all things common." The phrase "all things common" is a translation of the Greek word *koinonia*. It means that they shared everything. The same phrase is used in Acts 4:32: "And the multitude of them that believed were of one heart and of one soul: neither said any of them that ought of the things which he possessed was his own; but they had all things common."

The church is a loving, caring community of believers. Anything that damages or destroys the communion of saints is sin. The Holy Spirit is the chief architect of this fellowship. He ever brings unity and love to true believers. The scandalous splits in the church are a sad commentary upon the lack of the ministry of the Spirit in the life of the church.

True manifestation gifts will restore and strengthen the communion of saints. Believers will be bound together, and the joints which unite them will be strengthened. The ligaments will be strengthened, and the members will function together more effectively. This is a basic guideline for the manifestations of the Spirit. So when the supernatural manifestations are given to the church, there should be greater unity and love than ever before.

COMPASSION

In Matthew 9:36 we read: "But when he saw the multitudes, he was moved with compassion on them, because they fainted, and were scattered abroad, as sheep having no shepherd." Jesus looked at the masses of people and saw sheep. They were not yet His, but He viewed them with the eye of faith. He knew that potentially they were the sons of God; potentially they belonged to the flock of God. And as He looked, His heart went out to them. How important it is to remember that the ultimate purpose of the church is to evangelize, to win men to faith in Jesus Christ. When the Spirit of God is moving and the manifestations of the Spirit are being given in the church, compassion for the lost will be fanned to a white heat. The church will be delivered from self-centeredness and propelled into self-giving witness.

There are churches where the people become obsessed with spiritual gifts and totally engrossed in ministering to one another. There is no outreach. There is no evangelistic ministry. The people are selfishly reveling in spiritual gifts. Something is wrong with that kind of preoccupation with spiritual gifts. The ministry of the Spirit will evangelize. The ultimate purpose of the church's existence in the world is to evangelize the world—to make Christ known to the nations.

These five guidelines emphasize five basic truths of the church:

(1) Christ is the chief cornerstone of the church. He is the foundation. No other foundation can any lay than that which is laid, which is Christ Jesus (1 Corinthians 3:11). Christ must be at the center of spiritual gifts. He is not on the

periphery. The ministry of the Spirit is not something different from the ministry of the Lord Jesus Christ. There are three persons in the Trinity, but there is only one God. When the Spirit speaks, it is Christ speaking. Jesus said, "...he that hath seen me hath seen the Father..." (John 14:9).

And we could go further, and say that when the Holy Spirit comes, you will know that Jesus has come. For He is the fullness of the Godhead spiritually, just as Jesus is the fullness of the Godhead bodily. God the Father, God the Son, and God the Holy Spirit are three persons, but there is one God in those three persons. The ministry of the Spirit is in complete harmony with the ministry of Christ. The redemptive work of the Lord Jesus Christ is confirmed and completed in the work of the Spirit.

(2) The canon is the final authority for the church. The infallible Word must ever be the final court of appeal in all questions of both doctrine and conduct.

So in the first two guidelines we have the cornerstone and the canon—Christ and the Scriptures. These are vital truths for the life of the church.

In the final three guidelines we have the threefold ministry of the church—worship, fellowship, and witness.

(3) Celebration is the church worshiping her living Lord.

(4) Communion is the church sharing the life of her living Lord.

(5) Compassion is the church proclaiming her living Lord.

This threefold ministry is essential to the life and health of the church. Furthermore, these ministries flow in a divinely appointed order. We start with worship—celebration. We cannot start anyplace else. From true worship the church flows into the communion of saints. When we love God as we ought, it is natural to love our brother. The love of God is shed abroad in our hearts (Romans 5:5), and flows automatically into our relationships with our brethren. This flow then continues until it reaches out to the world in compassionate witness.

And so, we have five guidelines for measuring spiritual manifestations. All manifestations can be judged by applying these guidelines to them. If the manifestations do not pass these tests, then the church may need some pastoral and prophetic correction. In a sense, the variety of spiritual gifts tends to maintain guard over each other.

For example, the manifestation gift of the discerning of spirits will reveal to the church the source of other manifestations. It will identify the source of the manifestation as either divine, demonic, or human. We must not fall into the trap of thinking that every manifestation is either divine or demonic. Many spiritual manifestations are more human spirit than they are either divine or demonic.

We must be aware of these three sources of manifestations. That is the reason we need the guidelines.

According to Paul's exhortation in 1 Corinthians 14:39, manifestations must be judged. He provides some wise counsel in this chapter. This, along with other passages, provides the bases for these guidelines. We use five words: *Christ, canon, celebration, communion, compassion.* Christ is central. The canon is the final rule and authority. Celebration is the church at worship. The communion of saints is the body of Christ sharing His life with one another. Compassion is the church entering into the reality of John 3:16. May God help us to know how to judge and evaluate spiritual manifestations so as to guarantee that they will be genuine and continuing.

STUDY QUESTIONS FOR CHAPTER

1. Where should one go to find the biblical guidelines for spiritual manifestations?

2. List five words that may be used to judge manifestation gifts.

3. What does the word *canon* mean?

4. Who is primarily responsible for applying biblical guidelines to manifestations?

◆

CHAPTER TEN

The Greatest Hindrance– The Flesh

A nyone who deals seriously with the subject of spiritual gifts must come face to face with the greatest hindrance to spiritual gifts. This enemy is identified clearly in Galatians 5. Beginning with verse 13 we read:

For you were called to freedom, brethren; only do not turn your freedom into an opportunity for the flesh, but through love serve one another. For the whole Law is fulfilled in one word, in the statement, "You shall love your neighbor as yourself." But if you bite and devour one another, take care lest you be consumed by one another. But I say, walk by the Spirit, and you will not carry out the desire of the flesh. For the flesh sets its desire against the Spirit, and the Spirit against the flesh; for these are in opposition to one another, so that you may not do the things that you please. But if you are led by the Spirit, you are not under the Law. Now the deeds of the flesh are evident, which are: immorality, impurity, sensuality, idolatry, sorcery, enmities, strife, jealousy, outbursts of anger, disputes, dissensions, factions, envyings, drunkenness, carousing, and things like these, of which I forewarn you just as I have forewarned you that those who practice such things shall not inherit the kingdom of God. But the fruit of the Spirit is love, joy, peace, patience, kindness, goodness, faithfulness, gentleness, self-control; against such things there is no law. Now those who belong to Christ Jesus have crucified the flesh with its passions and desires. If we live by the Spirit, let us also walk by the Spirit. Let us not become boastful, challenging one another, envying one another (vv. 13-26, NASB).

DEFINITION

The enemy of the Spirit is the *flesh*. The desires of the flesh are hostile to the Holy Spirit, and the desires of the Spirit are hostile to the flesh.

When Paul uses the word *flesh,* he is not referring to our physical bodies. For Paul, man is spirit, soul, and body—*pneuma, psuche,* and *soma.* But the flesh is not to be identified with either of these. The flesh is not an essential part of man's nature as God created him. Paul uses the Greek word *sarx* to identify this enemy.

Man's spirit is his God-consciousness—that part of man that communes with God, the Eternal Spirit. The soul is the seat of man's self-consciousness. It includes his intellect, his emotions, and his will. The body is man's vehicle of expressing himself to other men. The body may be an instrument for either the spirit or the soul. The flesh is the fallen nature of man; it involves spirit, soul, and body.

The flesh is that unregenerate nature of man that is prone to sin and is in rebellion against God. It is centered in the human self.

Nothing will hinder the work of the Spirit more than the works of the flesh. If the flesh is at work in the life of a church, the flesh will put out the fire of the Spirit. Paul identifies the flesh as the culprit in the church at Corinth (1 Corinthians 3:1-3).

Another term used by Paul is "old man" (Romans 6:6; Ephesians 4:22; Colossians 3:9). This "old man" is to be crucified. He is to be "put off." He is the great enemy of the "new man" in Christ. The work of the Holy Spirit is to bring the "new man" into the full stature of Christian maturity. The "old man" opposes that purpose with unyielding hostility.

WORKS OF THE FLESH

Paul lists the works of the flesh in Galatians 5:19-21. The *New American Standard Bible* and many other translations list fifteen works of the flesh. Seventeen are listed in the *King James Version.* The translators in 1611 used two English words for one Greek word in some cases. But using the fifteen words that are found in the *New American Standard Bible,* Paul defines four categories of the works of the flesh: (1) *works in the sexual realm;* (2) *works in the spiritual realm;* (3) *works in the social realm;* and (4) *works in the realm of self-indulgence.*

(1) Works in the Sexual Realm.

Three works may be categorized in the sexual realm:

a. Immorality. The *King James Version* reads "fornication." The word Paul uses includes both adultery and fornication. It is really a comprehensive term referring to any act that abuses the sexuality of man. Therefore it is acts of immorality.

b. Impurity. Another translation reads "dirty-mindedness." The word in the Greek describes one who becomes obsessed with immorality. He not only commits deeds of immorality, but he thinks about it all the time. "Dirty-mindedness" is a good translation. Surely we ought to know what that is in our day. Dirty-mindedness is one of the most shocking characteristics of our society, and it is being exported around the world by means of television, movies, and internet. It has become popular in our society to use sexual immorality as the core of both comedy and commerce. We even try to sell toothpaste by parading sex. Our society is so sex-soaked that most everything seems to be oriented in that direction.

Popular comedy shows on television are filled with off-color jokes. The more risque the program, the better raves they get in the newspaper reviews. Why? Because we are a dirty-minded people.

c. Sensuality. The *Revised Standard Version* reads "licentiousness." *The New International Version* gives "debauchery."

The *Jerusalem Bible* renders it "sexual irresponsibility." The Greek word means to become blatantly open with immorality. It is immorality that parades itself without shame. It is a point in human behavior where men not only live immoral, dirty-minded lives, but they hang that depravity out for the whole world to see.

Paul presents the progressively more blatant violations of man's sexuality, starting with immorality, moving on to dirty-mindedness, and finally reaching the point of brazen licentiousness. These are the three works in the realm of sexuality.

(2) Works in the Spiritual Realm.

Paul lists two works in this category:

(a) Idolatry. Idolatry is the worship of false gods represented by manmade images. The pagans were known for their idolatry. We may feel that modern Western civilization is free from this work of the flesh, but we have our own deadly, sophisticated manifestation of idolatry. We worship possessions, positions, status symbols, and even sex. Idolatry is worshiping anything other than the true God. "God is a Spirit: and they that worship him must worship him in spirit and in truth" (John 4:24).

This manifestation of the flesh focuses on man's desire to have a physical representation of God. Man hungers to see God, to know God, to have a god who can be comprehended by the human senses. This is evident in Exodus 32:1-6 when, after having been marvelously delivered by Jehovah God, Israel longed to have an image of that God. Aaron took gold earrings that the people had collected in Egypt and made a golden calf to represent Jehovah. God forbade any man to make images because there was coming a day when God was going to reveal His Image to man. We now have an Image of God, the Lord Jesus Christ. He is the Image of the Invisible God. There is to be no other. Furthermore, man was totally incapable of designing any image that would represent Jehovah God. But man seems bent on devising all kinds of idolatry or false worship.

b. Sorcery. The second work of the flesh in the spiritual realm is "sorcery." The *King James Version* reads "witchcraft." The word in the Greek is *pharmakeia,* from which we get our word *pharmacy.* The word denotes the use of drugs in worship. The modern drug culture is basically a spiritual movement, an effort to get in tune with spiritual realities through the use of drugs. This is not a new manifestation, but it has exploded into a major human problem. It is a false movement. It is leading millions of deluded people into slavery and ruin.

(3) Works of the Social Realm.

This third category of the works of the flesh is the largest. More things are listed in this category than in all of the others put together. Whereas three works are named in the sexual realm and two in the spiritual realm, eight are listed in the *social realm.* All of these strike at the unity of the church.

The eight are *enmities, strife, jealousy, outbursts of anger, disputes, dissensions, factions, envyings.* These works are at the core of Paul's description of the activities of the "old man." They vividly portray the lifestyle of those who are the greatest enemies of the ministry of the Spirit in the church. Let us look at these eight words.

(a) Enmities. The *King James Version* reads "hatred." The *Revised Standard Version* renders it "hostility." The Greek word for enemy is *echthros.* The word here is *echthra.* Thus, it is the attitude of an enemy. It is the show of hostility toward another person.

(b) Strife. The *New English Bible* reads "a contentious temper." While enmity is the attitude of mind toward another person, strife is the outworking of that attitude.

(c) Jealousy. The Greek word is *zelos.* In its evil sense, as it is used here, it means resentment against others who are enjoying good fortune and blessing. This word is also used in a good sense to mean zeal, such as being zealous for spiritual gifts (1 Corinthians 14:12). But here it means jealousy.

(d) Outbursts of anger. The *New English Bible* gives "fits of rage." The Greek word *thumas* may be used for either good or evil anger. It is used seven times in the book of Revelation to refer to the wrath of God. But mostly it is used in an evil sense to refer to agitated outbursts of anger.

(e) Disputes. The *New International Version* gives "selfish ambition." Barclay says, "It describes a wrong attitude in the doing of work and in the holding of office" (*Flesh and Spirit,* p. 54).

(f) Dissensions. The Greek word *dichostasia* means literally "a standing apart." It means division. It is the dividing of people and groups of people.

(g) Factions. The Greek word is *haireseis* from which we get our word "heresy." This brings division to a point that people have to choose between two parties.

(h) Envyings. The difference between jealousy and envy is that jealousy resents what others possess, while envy wants to *take* what belongs to others.

These eight works of the flesh in the social realm are listed along with adultery and idolatry as enemies of the Spirit.

Some may resent the fact that Paul throws jealously into the same category as licentiousness and sorcery. But these eight works in the social realm do more to hinder the cause of Christ than do the grosser works in the sexual realm.

(4) Works in the Realm of Self-Indulgence.

The final two works of the flesh, drunkenness and carousings, are in the realm of self-indulgence. The church has done fairly well in protecting itself from the works of the flesh in the sexual realm, the spiritual realm, and the self-indulgence realm, but the havoc in the church has been wrought primarily by the eight works in the social realm. The Holy Spirit has been hindered repeatedly in His ministry by the jealousies, divisions, envyings, and fits of rage in the body of Christ. The flesh is hostile to the Spirit. The flesh is the enemy of the gifts and ministries of the Spirit.

The gifts of the Spirit are given to us to enable us to minister to other members of the body of Christ. The life of God flows from one member to another according to grace given to each one. Any disruption of the lines of communication between members is deadly. The flesh is the chief culprit in this disruption. All the eight works of the flesh in the social realm are aimed at destroying the unity of the body of Christ. In God's sight these works are just as heinous as adultery and drunkenness. It is a commentary on the church's spiritual perception that she has seldom shared this view. When one truly perceives the unity of the Body and the mutuality of spiritual gifts, it is then easy to see the flesh as the deadly enemy of the Spirit.

CRUCIFY THE FLESH

It is important that we deal with the flesh. No believer can have the fullness of the Spirit of God if he does not deal with the flesh. What are we to do with the flesh—the old man? Galatians 5:24 provides the answer: "Now those who belong to Christ Jesus have crucified the flesh with its passions and desires" (NASB). In Romans 6:6, Paul declares, "knowing this, that our old self was crucified with Him...." This means that the provision has been made in the death of the Lord Jesus Christ for the flesh to be crucified. Our old nature was crucified with Him on the cross. Now it is necessary for us to appropriate this by faith. The believer is exhorted in Romans 6 :11, "Even so consider yourselves to be dead to sin, but alive to God in Christ Jesus" (NASB).

It is expressed another way in Ephesians 4:22, 23: " . . . in reference to your former manner of life, you lay aside the old self, which is being corrupted in accordance with the lusts of deceit, and that you be renewed in the spirit of your mind ...." In Colossians 3:9, 10 we are exhorted, "Do not lie to one another, since you laid aside the old self with its evil practices, and have put on the new self who is being renewed to a true knowledge according to the image of the One who created him" (NASB).

And so it is essential for the Christian, if he is to be spiritual and enjoy the gifts of the Spirit, that the old man be crucified. He must be put to death. Sensitivity to the Spirit requires that one be dead to the works of the flesh.

The first step which must be taken in many churches and in many believers, if they are to attain to a full-orbed spiritual life, is the crucifixion of the old man. John Wesley called it "entire sanctification." Any biblical doctrine of sanctification must embrace this crucifixion of the flesh.

This takes place in the believer when he reckons himself to be dead to sin, but alive unto God. The work has been accomplished in the crucifixion of Christ, and the believer must identify with Him in this crucifixion. In so doing, he will remove the greatest hindrance to the manifestation of the Spirit.

STUDY QUESTIONS FOR CHAPTER 10

1. What is the greatest enemy of the ministry of the Spirit?

2. In what four areas does this enemy work?

3. Which area seems to be the most important foothold of this enemy?

4. What can be done with this enemy of the Spirit?

CHAPTER ELEVEN

———————◆———————

The Atmosphere of the Gifts– The Fruit of the Spirit

In order to grow oranges or peaches, one must be located in a climate conducive to the growth of these fruits. Spiritual gifts also develop and operate best in the proper climate. The atmosphere in some churches is such that spiritual manifestations are killed by "frostbite."

In this chapter, we will look at the atmosphere for the gifts, the atmosphere conducive to the functioning of both the ministry gifts and the manifestation gifts of the Spirit. Let us turn again to Galatians, chapter 5, and focus attention on the ninefold fruit of the Spirit listed in verses 22 and 23: "But the fruit of the Spirit is love, joy, peace, patience, kindness, goodness, faithfulness, gentleness, self-control; against such things there is no law" (NASB). We must emphasize the fact that in order for a church to be healthy, it must have ministry gifts, manifestation gifts, and the fruit of the Spirit. It is impossible for the church to be what she ought to be if any of these things are missing.

Some would emphasize the fruit, but neglect the gifts of the Spirit. Others might emphasize the gifts of the Spirit, while completely ignoring the fruit of the Spirit. In reality, we do not have a choice. When we receive the Holy Spirit, we should receive His multifaceted ministry. We should receive His ministry gifts, which He bestows upon the members of the body of Christ. We also should be open to receive the manifestations of the Spirit—the surprises of the Spirit—

113

which are a vital part of His ministry, and we should receive the fruit of the Spirit. How can one receive the Holy Spirit while rejecting part of His ministry? All of these are essential to the health and well-being of the church.

The manifestation gifts are temporary, supernatural revelations of the Spirit's presence, while the fruit of the Spirit is to become increasingly a permanent part of the lifestyle of God's people. Furthermore, the ninefold fruit is like a flower. One does not "shop" for one or two of these traits while ignoring the others. These are not various options for the believer. Rather, they are part of a divine package. If we accept the Spirit in His fullness, the fruit will naturally follow, for this fruit of the Spirit is the climate, the atmosphere, in which the Holy Spirit can operate. Those who would desire spiritual gifts should study the fruit of the Spirit as the climate in which the Holy Spirit operates.

Let us examine individually these nine aspects of the fruit of the Spirit.

LOVE

The Greek word is *agape*. William Barclay defines *agape* as "unconquerable benevolence, invincible good will." This is that quality of love that God has for sinful man. It is the ability to love the unlovable. It is that unconquerable good will that is part of the life of a Christian. It can be produced only by the Holy Spirit in the life of a believer.

There are four words for love in the Greek: *Eros* means erotic love, sensual love. *Phileo* refers to tender affection and was the highest word for love in secular Greek usage. *Storge* refers to family love. It was used to denote a mother's love for her children or the children's love for their parents. This is the love of kinship.

Agape, however, was seldom used in classical Greek, but it was taken up by the New Testament writers and given special definition. It refers to the love that God has for us. A love that refuses to be defeated. The definition of this word must be drawn from its New Testament usage.

Agape is shed abroad in the heart of the Christian by the

Holy Spirit (Romans 5:5). G. Campbell Morgan held that *agape* is the *fruit* of the Spirit (singular). All other traits which follow are but expressions of *agape.*

JOY

The Greek word *chara,* as it is used in the New Testament, means joy because of being reconciled to God and received as sons. It is the joy of the Lord—the joy that comes from knowing that you are accepted in the Beloved. That joy is accentuated, strengthened, and ripened by the ministry of the Spirit. Joy "unspeakable and full of glory" is characteristic of true Christians. This is such a contradiction to some manifestations of Christianity. I've seen some people who believe very strongly that the more Christian you are, the sadder or more melancholy you are.

This sad, long-faced concept of Christianity is opposite to what the New Testament teaches. The fruit of the Spirit is *joy.* Paul says again and again, "Rejoice." He wrote the Philippian letter while in prison. While chained to Roman soldiers in a damp prison, he wrote: "Rejoice in the Lord always: and again I say, Rejoice" (Philippians 4:4). Joy is the fruit of the Spirit, and it ought to be characteristic of every Christian—especially of Spirit-filled Christians.

PEACE

The Greek word here is *eirene,* meaning tranquility of mind based on the consciousness of a right relation to God. This tranquility comes to us because we know that we are at peace with God. There is no more conflict in our lives against God; no more war with Him; we have laid down our weapons of warfare. Our wills have been completely surrendered to His will, and this brings perfect peace.

LONG-SUFFERING

Long-suffering is the opposite of short-temperedness. The *New International Commentary* comments that this word assumes attack, provocation and incentive to wrath. This word means patience and long-suffering while being provoked by an enemy.

Only the Spirit can produce such an attitude in the life of the Christian. Any person full of the Spirit will be a patient person, not given to short-temperedness. Ephesians 4:2 says: "...be patient, bearing with one another in love" (NIV). This is long-suffering. It is characteristic of Spirit-filled people.

KINDNESS

As Plummer defines it, kindness is "the sympathetic kindliness or sweetness of temper which puts others at their ease and shrinks from giving pain." This is that disposition that makes people comfortable in our presence. Some think that kindness is a sign of weakness and that to be hard and harsh and unkind is a sign of strength. But if you study the greatest and strongest Man who ever lived, Jesus Christ, you will see a kind Man. Little children saw His kindness and loved Him. Prostitutes and tax collectors saw His kindness and sought His company. One of the great differences between Jesus and many of His followers is in the attitude toward sinners. Sinners loved to be with Jesus because He was such a kind person. He had the fruit of the Spirit in full-blown manifestation without limitation. He is our pattern. And He was a friend of sinners. This was one of the chief accusations against Him by the Scribes and Pharisees.

GOODNESS

The Greek word is *agathosune.* Barclay defines it as "generous goodness." He says, "The great characteristic of *agathosune* is the generosity which gives man what he never could have earned." The basic idea is generosity. This is contrary to the world's greedy, grasping attitude that ever seeks to get.

The true Christian is more interested in giving than getting. Giving is the very nature of God. He freely gave His only begotten Son. His children share this nature. This generosity does not see how little it can give and be pleasing to

God, but how much it can give. And that generosity is willing to give to people who do not deserve it. Often we want people to merit the gift before we give. That is not the nature of the person with this generous goodness—a fruit of the Spirit.

FAITHFULNESS

The word "faith" in the KJV is not the best translation. The *New King James Version,* as well as the NASB and the RSV render it "faithfulness." Phillips renders it "fidelity." Barclay calls this "the virtue of reliability."

This certainly raises serious doubts about those who embrace a charismatic experience which leads to unfaithfulness. Before their so-called pentecostal experience they were dependable, faithful members of a body of believers. After this experience they become spiritual gadflies running from one special meeting to another. They no longer can be depended upon by any congregation of believers. They have no faithfulness in ministering to the body of Christ. They become unreliable, spiritual thrill-seekers. Dependability is the one ability without which all other abilities are useless.

The Holy Spirit instills faithfulness into those whom He equips for ministry in the church.

One of the greatest griefs of pastors is watching members of the church with great ability, people with spiritual gifts as teachers and administrators, etc., who cannot be depended on to be faithful in their ministry.

The Holy Spirit does not give spiritual gifts to produce spiritual gadabouts. The manifestations of the Spirit ought to be bathed in this atmosphere of faithfulness.

The manifestations of the Spirit should come to a congregation largely, if not solely, through members who are faithful to that congregation. Any word from a prophet or evangelist who is unknown to the congregation should be examined carefully. Generally, the Holy Spirit will use faithful, dependable members of the congregation through whom to work. Reliability! Dependability! Faithfulness! This is a fruit of the Spirit.

MEEKNESS

Probably no other manifestation of the fruit of the Spirit is more misunderstood than meekness. Aristotle said that meekness was the mean between too much and too little anger. The meek man gets angry at the right time, over the right things, and for the right length of time. As a young Christian I heard that a person who was really sanctified never got angry. Anger was supposed to be removed by the crucifixion of the old man. But when I read that Jesus was angry (Mark 3:5) and that He drove the money changers from the Temple (Matthew 21:12, 13), I had to reexamine that premise. Anger is a God-given capacity. God Himself is capable of anger (Psalm 7:11; 2 Kings 22:13; Ezra 8:22). Meekness is that God-given ability to so master the capacity for anger that one is angry at the right time and for the right reason and for the right length of time.

Meekness has often been misunderstood as weakness, the "doormat complex." The trait was represented in a person with little ability and little ambition, one who was willing to let everybody run over him because he had no other alternative. He was soft-spoken and easy-going, and anybody could take advantage of him.

That is not what this word means. The Holy Spirit does not create duplicates of Casper Milquetoast. In fact, the word that is used here in the Greek, *prautes,* is a term that was used for a high-spirited horse that had been well trained. The picture is of a strong, muscular, Arabian steed. With bowed neck and prancing feet he awaits the command of his master. He could go in any direction and the rider could do nothing about it, but the rider tugs to the right and the horse goes to the right. He pulls the reign to the left and the horse goes to the left. He gives a slight pull and the horse stops. He touches the flanks and all of the massive strength of that animal goes into action in response to the touch of the master.

In other words, it is a picture of strength under control, power under discipline. Meekness is not weakness. It is strength, but strength that is under control; strength that is in submission to the Master. Meekness is an attitude toward

God that says all of my powers, all of my abilities are under submission to God. And if God puts me in submission to someone else, as far as the ministry of the church is concerned, I can submit my power (spiritually, mentally, physically) to that authority. I have strength and ability to act, but it is under control.

Jesus personifies meekness. He said, "I am meek and lowly in heart: and ye shall find rest unto your souls" (Matthew 11:29b).

Jesus was not a weak man. He was the strongest man who ever lived, but He was meek. He was under the total authority of His Father. He sought only to do His Father's will. His power was in submission to the Father.

And so meekness is that fruit of the Spirit that helps us to keep our strength under control, especially our capacity for anger. A meek man does not have fits of rage—that is the work of the flesh. He does not get angry for selfish reasons. Jesus never got angry because of what people did to Him. He got angry because of what they were doing to other people. It was an unselfish anger.

SELF-CONTROL

The word *temperance* is better translated "self-control." This is victory over desire. William Barclay says, "The opposite of *egkrateia* is action dominated by desire, and the man who is *egkrates* is the man who prevents desire from being the dictator of his actions and his life" (*Flesh and Spirit,* p. 126). This trait runs counter to modern humanistic philosophy, but it is the lifestyle of the Spirit-filled believer. Spiritual gifts are at home in the atmosphere of self-control.

Only the Holy Spirit can create the climate in which both ministry gifts and manifestation gifts can flourish and thus minister to a healthy, growing church. This climate is called "the fruit of the Spirit."

This ninefold fruit creates an atmosphere in which the Spirit of God can move. The ministry gifts can be developed and deployed without the hindrance of the works of the flesh. The manifestation gifts can flow freely as the Spirit wills.

Thus, the church will grow and reproduce itself in a normal New Testament pattern.

Remember, it is not the gifts *or* the fruit. It is both —the gifts *and* the fruit: ministry gifts, manifestation gifts, and the fruit of the Spirit—blended together in the life of the Spirit.

STUDY QUESTIONS FOR CHAPTER 11

1. List the ninefold fruit of the Spirit.

2. What are the four words for love in the Greek language? Define briefly.

3. What is meekness?

4. What three elements of the Spirit's ministry are blended in the life of the church?

CHAPTER TWELVE

◆

The Most Important Ingredient In Spiritual Gifts – Love

We began our study by making a distinction between ministry gifts and manifestation gifts. We then defined twenty spiritual gifts—four equipping ministry gifts, seven body ministry gifts, and nine manifestation gifts. We have discussed the harmonizing of the gifts and guidelines for judging the manifestation gifts. In the two immediately preceding chapters we have identified the greatest enemy of spiritual gifts and the atmosphere in which spiritual gifts can function most effectively.

In this final chapter we want to look at the most important ingredient of spiritual gifts. It is so vital that we might call it "the glue of the gifts."

This ingredient is easily identified by reading carefully the primary passages in our study of spiritual gifts. Let us go back to Romans 12, 1 Corinthians 12, Ephesians 4, and 1 Peter 4. When we examine these passages carefully, we find that each of them contains a strong exhortation to *love* the brethren.

In Romans 12:6-8 Paul identifies seven spiritual gifts and gives brief instruction on how each is to be exercised in the church. But immediately following this list, in verse nine, he says, "Let love be without dissimulation." Or, as the *New*

International Version reads, "Love must be sincere." Verse ten continues this exhortation, "Be kindly affectioned one to another with brotherly love; in honour preferring one another." The NIV gives, "Be devoted to one another in brotherly love." In other words, the apostle is saying, "Let love be genuine and without pretense. And let this love be the bond that ties you to your brothers."

The context in 1 Corinthians 12 is even stronger. Paul concludes the chapter: "But covet earnestly the best gifts: and yet shew I unto you a more excellent way" (v. 31). Then follows that peerless passage on love in Chapter 13. (It is significant that the greatest passage ever penned on love comes in connection with this Scriptural section on spiritual gifts.) Paul then opens chapter fourteen with the words, "Pursue this love" (Barclay). The pursuit of love must exceed even the desire for spiritual gifts.

In Ephesians 4 the same emphasis is found. The chapter begins with an exhortation to love. "I therefore, the prisoner of the Lord, beseech you that ye walk worthy of the vocation wherewith ye are called, With all lowliness and meekness, with longsuffering, **forbearing one another in love***; Endeavoring to keep the unity of the Spirit in the bond of peace" (vv. 1-3). Note how this unity in love is coupled with the Spirit in verse three. It is only in the full-orbed ministry of the Holy Spirit that true unity can exist in the church. It is the Spirit who is at work when the love of God is shed abroad in our hearts (Romans 5:5).

After presenting the sevenfold unity of the church, Paul lists and defines the work of the equipping ministry gifts in the church. He closes this passage with verse sixteen. In fact, verse fifteen describes this ministry as "speaking the truth **in love**"* (Ephesians 4:15).

But then he concludes: "from whom the whole body, being fitted and held together by that which every joint supplies, according to the proper working of each individual part, causes the growth of the body for the **building up of itself in love**"* (NASB). The emphasis is upon love. The building

*Emphasis mine

124

of the body of Christ must be done in the context of love.

The final passage on spiritual gifts was found in 1 Peter 4. Verses 10 and 11 are key verses in studying this subject. Verse 10 makes clear that every member of the body of Christ is given a gift. Verse eleven tells how it is to be exercised. But in verse 8 we read, "Above all, keep fervent **in your love for one another**,* because love covers a multitude of sins" (NASB). It is clear that Peter is giving top priority to love. He says, "**above all**,* love each other deeply" (NIV). Love is the most important ingredient in the exercising of spiritual gifts.

For the most powerful presentation of this truth, we must turn to that majestic 13th chapter of 1 Corinthians. Don't ever forget that the greatest passage ever written on love is in the midst of Paul's greatest discourse on spiritual gifts. In fact, 1 Corinthians 12-14 is by far the most important passage in the Bible on spiritual gifts. Sandwiched into this great passage is Paul's song to love. A careful examination of this chapter should be a fitting conclusion to our study of spiritual gifts.

Someone has said that every Christian should take a bath in this chapter at least once a month. So just in case you haven't had your bath in 1 Corinthians 13 this month, let us read it together:

> If I speak with the tongues of men and of angels, but do not have love, I have become a noisy gong or a clanging cymbal. And if I have the gift of prophecy, and know all mysteries and all knowledge; and if I have all faith, so as to remove mountains, but do not have love, I am nothing. And if I give all my possessions to feed the poor and if I deliver my body to be burned, but do not have love, it profits me nothing.

> Love is patient, love is kind, and is not jealous; love does not brag and is not arrogant, does not act unbecomingly; it does not seek its own, is not provoked, does not take into account a wrong suffered, does not rejoice in unrighteousness, but rejoices with the

*Emphasis mine

truth; bears all things, believes all things, hopes all things, endures all things.

Love never fails; but if there are gifts of prophecy, they will be done away; if there are tongues, they will cease; if there is knowledge, it will be done away. For we know in part, and we prophesy in part; but when the perfect comes, the partial will be done away.

When I was a child, I used to speak as a child, think as a child, reason as a child; when I became a man, I did away with childish things. For now we see in a mirror dimly, but then face to face; now I know in part, but then I shall know fully just as I also have been fully known.

But now abide faith, hope, love, these three; but the greatest of these is love (NASB).

At the heart of any study of spiritual gifts, if it is to be biblical, must be this vital subject of divine love. And no such study could be complete without a careful look at 1 Corinthians 13.

PERFECTION OF LOVE

We may divide the chapter into three sections. The first three verses picture for us *the perfection of love*. We may look at these verses as if they were mathematical equations. The first equation is Tongues minus Love equals Senseless Noise (Tongues − Love = Senseless Noise). What a formula! Tongues is the gift of tongues, or the manifestation of tongues. Paul is saying emphatically that unless love is the motivation and atmosphere for the manifestation of tongues, the manifestation is worthless. It is no more than an annoying noise.

The second equation is Prophecy minus Love equals Zero (Prophecy − Love = 0). The lack of love cancels out any value there is in prophecy. This clearly establishes the truth that love must be the motivation for prophetic utterances.

The third equation is Wisdom to the nth degree plus Knowledge to the nth degree minus Love equals Zero (Or

Knowledge$^{\circ\circ}$ + Wisdom$^{\circ\circ}$ − Love = 0). Considering the context of this passage, it seems certain that Paul is referring to the manifestation gifts of a word of wisdom and a word of knowledge.

The fourth equation reads: Giving to the nth degree plus Martyrdom minus Love equals Zero (Giving$^{\circ\circ}$ + Martyrdom − Love = 0).

These four equations clearly emphasize the importance of love. But, in the light of the entire passage on gifts, we also could draw up some positive equations:

(1) Tongues plus Love equals Edification (Tongues + Love = Edification). Read 1 Corinthians 14:4, 5.

(2) Prophecy plus Love equals Edification and Evangelism (Prophecy + Love = Edification + Evangelism). Read 1 Corinthians 14:3,12, 24, 25.

(3) Wisdom plus Knowledge plus Love equals Church Growth (Wisdom + Knowledge + Love = Church Growth).

(4) Giving plus Love equals Riches in Heaven and Church Growth (Giving + Love = Riches in Heaven + Church Growth).

As we examine the teaching of the New Testament, these equations are clearly true. Such passages as Matthew 6:1-4 support this. Without love all spiritual gifts are worthless. But when love is added, all gifts are brought to perfection. When this most important ingredient is added, the results are amazing. Spiritual gifts then become powerful instruments in the building of the church.

PORTRAIT OF LOVE

The second section of this tremendous chapter (vv. 4-7) presents a *portrait of love.* Paul describes love in both positive and negative statements.

Negatively, he lists eight statements that tell us what love is not. He also makes seven positive statements. So, the apostle thinks that it is important to know what love is not, as well as what it is. The negative statements all point to works of the flesh. Love will eliminate the work of the flesh. Jealousy is banished. Boasting is cast out. Pride is crucified

Rudeness is eliminated. Selfishness is buried. Violent anger is no more. The unforgiving spirit is nailed to the cross. Revenge does not exist. All of these belong to the "old man," and he has been crucified. These dark shadows help to accentuate the beauty of the portrait presented by the positive statements.

Just as the negative description corresponds to the works of the flesh listed in Galatians 5, so the positive description corresponds to the fruit of the Spirit described in the same chapter.

Love is patient. Love is kind. Love is joyful. Love is tolerant. Love is trusting. Love is hopeful and optimistic. Love is meek. What a remarkable likeness is this portrait to Jesus. It describes Him exactly. No wonder! He is the perfect revelation of Divine Love. He is the perfect pattern.

All of these traits have to do with our relationships with others. Love must be manifested in relationships with others. That is why we are told that if a man says that he loves God and does not love his brother, he is a liar. The gifts of the Spirit are given to us that we might minister the multifaceted grace of God to others. No wonder *love* is the most important ingredient.

PERMANENCE OF LOVE

In verses 8-13, we have the final section—*the permanence of love*. The contrasts in this passage are between the passing and the permanent, the partial and the perfect, immaturity and maturity. He contrasts the temporary nature of the spiritual gifts with the eternal nature of love. The gifts of the Spirit, whether they be ministry gifts or manifestation gifts, are not for eternity. They are for time. They will not be needed when that which is perfect is come (v. 10). A time will come when there will be no need for prophecy or for any of the manifestations. We will be living in the bright light of God's presence—the Father, the Son, and the Spirit will be ever manifested.

With all of our learning and understanding of the truth, the best informed of us have only partial perception of God and His purposes. One may study the Bible for a lifetime, but his understanding of God's Word will still be short of perfect. A student of the Bible is ever discovering "new" truths in God's revelation—truths which he has failed to see previously though they were there all the time. How partial is our spiritual perception! One may read a passage and think to himself, "When did that get in the Bible?" It was there all the time. His perception had not picked it up. He had not been able to see what God was saying. So, even our grasp of God's revealed Word is ever partial. But, in addition, God has not revealed to us all things in Scripture because they must await the day when we shall know even as we are known.

Of course, the basis of our need for spiritual gifts is our immaturity. The whole purpose of the equipping ministry gifts is to bring the church to maturity. If the church were mature, there would be no more need of apostles, prophets, evangelists, or pastor-teachers. There would be no need for any of the other spiritual gifts. Both ministry gifts and manifestation gifts would be obsolete.

The amazing thing is that some misunderstand this passage to mean that the supernatural manifestations of the Spirit have been withdrawn because that which is perfect has come. They hold that since we have the New Testament there is no more need for supernatural gifts.

The canon of Scripture is complete. But at the same time, the giving of this Bible did not bring the church to absolute perfection. It is not reasonable to take this passage to mean that the completion of the New Testament was the arrival of the perfection mentioned. Neither is it reasonable to hold that the possession of the New Testament brings us to the knowledge of ourselves as God knows us. It seems to be like the specious argument of someone who simply does not want to admit the possibility of the supernatural ministry of the Spirit.

Paul is not saying that supernatural gifts will pass away when the Scripture is completed. If that were true, why would it be necessary for Paul to write instructions concerning these surprises of the Spirit and give instruction and guidelines for their operation? The perfect has not yet come.

The gifts are still valid and present in the church. In fact, there seems to be a renewal of these manifestations as the church faces the challenge of the end time.

A time will come when all of these gifts will pass away. No more tongues. No more prophecy. No more healings. No more discerning of spirits, etc. But that will be when we have all come to the fullness of the stature of Christ. Only then will we no longer need the gifts of the Spirit which have been given to the church to equip her for her work of ministry. But even then love will abide. Love is a permanent thing. It will never, never cease.

Let us remember the *perfection of love,* the p*ortrait of love,* the *permanence of love.* This love is to permeate every ministry and every gift and every manifestation. Love is to be the atmosphere in which everything is done. Jesus said, "By this all men will know that you are My disciples, if you have love for one another" (John 13:35, NASB).

In conclusion to this study of spiritual gifts, let us unite in committing ourselves to the identifying and developing of our ministry gifts, becoming more sensitive and open to the manifestations of the Spirit, and cultivating the fruit of the Spirit which is the atmosphere of the gifts. May the Holy Spirit in all His multifaceted ministry work in us and through us to complete God's glorious purpose for us in Jesus Christ!

STUDY QUESTIONS FOR CHAPTER 12

1. What is the greatest chapter on love in the Bible? What is the context of this passage?

2. Give two equations that reveal the perfection of love.

3. Who is depicted in the Portrait of Love in 1 Corinthians 13:4-7?

4. What is the basis of the need for spiritual gifts?

BIBLIOGRAPHY

Barclay, William, *Daily Study Bible, The Letters To The Galatians And Ephesians,* Westminster, Washington, D.C., 1958.

_____, *Flesh and Spirit,* Abingdon Press, 1962.

Barrett, David, Editor, *The World Christian Encyclopedia,* Oxford University Press, Nashville, 1982.

Bruce, F. F., *The Book of Acts,* New International Commentary, William B. Eerdmans Publishing Co., Grand Rapids, 1960.

Ervin, Howard M., *These Are Not Drunken As Ye Suppose,* Logos International, Jacksonville, 1968.

Flynn, Leslie B., *19 Gifts of the Spirit,* Victor Books, Wheaton, 1978.

Frost, Robert, *Aglow with the Spirit,* Voice Christian Publications, 1965.

_____, *Set My Spirit Free,* Logos International, 1973.

Gee, Donald, *Concerning Spiritual Gifts,* Gospel Publishing House, Springfield, n.d.

_____, *Spiritual Gifts in the Work of the Ministry Today,* L.I.F.E. Bible College Alumni Association, 1963.

Green, Michael, *I Believe in the Holy Spirit,* Eerdmans Publishing Co., Grand Rapids, 1975.

Harper, Michael, *Let My People Grow,* Hodder and Stoughton, London, 1977.

Horton, Harold, *The Gifts of the Spirit,* Assemblies of God Publishing House, London, 1962.

Hummel, Charles E., *Fire in the Fireplace,* InterVarsity Press, Downers Grove, 1978.

King James Version, Oxford University Press, New York, 1967.

The Living Bible, Paraphrased, Tyndale House Publishers, Wheaton, 1973.

Mains, Karen Burton, *Open Heart—Open Home,* David C. Cook Publishing Co., Elgin, 1976.

McAlister, R. E., *The Manifestations of the Spirit,* n.p., n.d.

McRae, William, *The Dynamics of Spiritual Gifts,* Zondervan, Grand Rapids, 1976.

Morgan, G. Campbell, *The Westminster Pulpit,* Fleming H. Revell Co., Grand Rapids, 1955.

Moule, H. C. G., *Ephesian Studies,* Zondervan, Grand Rapids, n.d.

New American Standard Bible. Cambridge University Press, Cambridge, London, 1977.

New English Bible, Oxford University Press, New York, 1970.

New International Version, Zondervan Bible Publishers, Grand Rapids, 1978.

New King James Version, Thomas Nelson Publishers, Nashville, 1982.

Phillips, J. B. – *New Testament in Modern English,* Galahad Bks., N.Y., 1972.

Revised Standard Version, American Bible Society, New York, 1973.

Robertson, A. T., *Word Pictures in the New Testament, III,* Broadman Press, Nashville, 1930.

Sanders, Oswald J., *The Holy Spirit and His Gifts,* Zondervan, Grand Rapids, 1940.

Stedman, Ray C., *Body Life,* Regal Books, Ventura, 1972.

Strong, James, *Exhaustive Concordance of the Bible,* Abingdon, Nashville, 1980.

Thayer, J. H., *Greek-English Lexicon of the New Testament,* Zondervan, Grand Rapids, 1977.

Thomas, Robert L., *Understanding Spiritual Gifts,* Moody Press, Chicago, 1978.

Tuttle, Robert G., *The Partakers,* Pillar Books, Tulsa, 1974.

Underwood, B. E., *The Gifts of the Spirit*, Advocate Press, Franklin Springs, 1967.

Wagner, Peter, *Your Spiritual Gifts Can Help Your Church Grow,* Regal Books, Ventura, 1979.

Watson, David, *I Believe in the Church,* Hodder and Stoughton, London, 1978.

Wuest, Kenneth, *Word Studies In The New Testament-Ephesians,* Scripture Truth, Eerdmans Pub. Co., Grand Rapids, 1966.

Yohn, Rick, *Discover Your Spiritual Gift and Use It,* Tyndale House Publishers, Wheaton, 1976.